BUILDING THE FRAMEWORK

by
Clare Nankivell

From research by Clare Nankivell and Dr. Anna Frankel

The Basic Skills Agency

Acknowledgements

This report is the result of a research project undertaken by the Centre for Information Research and Training in the Faculty of Computing and Information Studies at the University of Central England in partnership with Bilston Community College in Wolverhampton. Professor Judith Elkin directed the project which was initially conceived by the Basic Skills Agency. Clare Nankivell and Dr. Kay Flatten managed the project from the University and Dr. Anna Frankel managed from the College. The project team would also like to thank Tony Bill, Liz Chilton, Anne Russell, Graham Taylor and the interview teams involved for their work on the project. We are grateful to Peter Shuker, Principal of Darlington College, Mike Bourke, Principal of Waltham Forest College and Keith Slater from Bournville College for their contribution as members of a Steering Committee.

Published March 1996

ISBN 1 85990 051 8

Design: Studio 21

Contents

Chapter 1: **Introduction**   5

Chapter 2: **The research sources**   8

Chapter 3: **National developments affecting basic skills support**   14

Chapter 4: **The wider picture of basic skills support in FE**   18

Chapter 5: **Case studies: policy and practice**   22

Chapter 6: **Effectiveness of basic skills support: completion and
achievement**   40

Chapter 7: **Conclusions**   47

Chapter 8: **References**   52

Appendices

Appendix I: Methodology   53

Appendix II: Staff Exercise:
           Section A   61
           Section B   79

Appendix III: Audit Instrument   82

CHAPTER 1

Introduction

The project

This report details the findings of an eighteen-month research project into the development of basic skills support in Further Education (FE) colleges in England and Wales. The research was commissioned by the Basic Skills Agency (formerly ALBSU) and conducted by the University of Central England (UCE) and Bilston Community College (BCC).

The Basic Skills Agency commissioned the research in response to studies showing that the levels of non-completion and of failure in FE were unacceptably high (e.g. Audit Commission, 1993). Previous research conducted for the Basic Skills Agency showed that a significant number of FE students needed support in communication or numeracy skills. The screening for basic skills need of over 10,000 students from 12 colleges suggested that many students did not have the requisite level of these skills to enable them to achieve qualifications. For example, the Basic Skills Agency believes that students functioning at Stage 1 (Basic Skills Agency Standards) in communication skills are likely to need basic skills support to achieve Level 2 NVQs. Results showed that 42% of students screened were at this level or lower. Some vocational areas had even higher proportions at this level, such as land based industries (46.4%), beauty/hairdressing (57.9%) and catering (56.6%). The report concluded 'it is likely that without additional support with basic skills many of these students will not successfully complete their course of study'. (ALBSU, 1993).

Taking the Basic Skills Agency's definition of basic skills support, the research team looked at how effective the whole process was in enabling students to 'progress and achieve a successful outcome on a vocational or academic course'. This involved looking at identification of need, through delivery to progress review and monitoring of students. Finally, the study drew conclusions about the factors involved in basic skills support and the experiences of the players involved – management, teaching staff and students.

What is basic skills support?

It is useful first to look at what basic skills are, before moving on to look at basic skills support and its role in FE. The Basic Skills Agency defines basic skills as:

'the ability to read, write and speak in English
and use mathematics at a level necessary to
function and progress at work and in society in general.'

'In Wales, basic skills includes the ability to read
and write Welsh for people whose first language
or mother tongue is Welsh.'
(ALBSU 1994)

Studies have repeatedly shown that a significant proportion of the adult population lacks these skills or has a very low level of proficiency in them (eg, Ekinsmyth and Bynner, 1994).

Basic skills support is additional help for students who may find their academic or vocational courses too difficult because of poor basic skills. The Basic Skills Agency defines it thus:

'Basic skills support is provided as part of some
other education or training provision in a college
and is usually concerned with helping students to
improve basic skills in order that they are able to
progress and achieve a successful outcome on a
vocational or academic course.'
(ALBSU 1994)

Basic skills support differs from primary basic skills programmes, often referred to as Adult Basic Education (ABE), in that the main aim of a student on a primary basic skills course is solely related to basic skills and the aim of a student receiving basic skills support is an academic or vocational qualification.

Nevertheless, basic skills support has grown out of primary programmes in many FE colleges and is often staffed by the same people, housed in the same accommodation and uses the same teaching materials and methods. The distinction between primary and support is not, therefore, clear cut in some colleges, particularly if students receiving support are also gaining accreditation for basic skills.

CHAPTER 2

The research sources

The research involved a number of surveys conducted in colleges between May 1994 and October 1995. These surveys were underpinned by a literature review conducted in Spring 1994. The methodology pursued in this research is detailed in Appendix I.

Large-scale surveys

Three surveys were undertaken of 206 colleges selected from the FEFC list of general and tertiary colleges as those providing basic skills support. These surveys were conducted by mailed questionnaire, sent directly to Principals or Chief Executives by name. The aim of the first two questionnaires, sent in June 1994 and May 1995, was to generate a picture of basic skills support in FE.

Those questionnaires focused on:

- methods of identifying basic skills support need
- enrolment and attendance figures and monitoring procedures
- college structure and delivery models
- student achievements
- staffing levels
- sources of data given.

Although the overall response rates to these questionnaires was good, many respondents were unable to answer specific questions and thus provide data the research team had aimed to collect. This was especially true for questions on student achievement and completion. For example, of the 130 respondents to the 1994 survey only 25 could provide the numbers of basic skills support students who achieved academic or vocational qualifications and only 39 reported that they could identify non-completion rates for basic skills support students. A supplementary questionnaire was mailed in Autumn 1994 to all those from the first survey who reported that they were able to identify non-completion rates. This asked for non-completion rates for basic skills support and non-basic skills support students. Very few responses to this questionnaire were received, and many did not in fact provide all the data requested.

The third survey of all 206 colleges in October 1995 asked ten questions on completion, withdrawal and achievement of students identified through screening or assessment as needing basic skills support.

Case studies

Eight colleges were selected as case studies. These eight colleges were selected to represent the variety in FE, such as size, socio-economic area, number of sites and length of time basic skills support had been established. The eight were from different geographical areas:

Yorkshire	Midlands
North East	South West
North West	South East
Wales	London.

Each of these colleges was studied in depth through interview surveys, observational audits and analysis of college documents collected by the audit team.

College profiles

This section briefly describes the colleges studied by type of area; size; numbers of staff and students involved in basic skills support; and the basic skills support history.

The first college was in a semi-rural tourist area. The college had five sites spread over a large area and over 3,000 full-time equivalent (FTE) students. Basic skills support was a very new development and was based on a model of a Central Resource Unit and individual departments or schools providing basic skills support. In 1993-94 seventy students received basic skills support. In 1994-95 the college appointed one full-time dedicated basic skills support tutor and three other full-time tutors were teaching basic skills support as part of their duties.

The second college was on city outskirts serving a wide community through five sites, and including a high proportion of students whose first language was not English. The college had nearly 6,000 FTE students. Basic skills support was a recent development, having grown out of the college's ABE department. It had 669 full-time students receiving basic skills support in 1994-95 from five dedicated part-time tutors and four full-time tutors who taught basic skills support as part of their responsibilities. ESOL (English for Speakers of Other Languages) provision was available on all the colleges' sites and was staffed by dedicated ESOL tutors.

The third college was in a town in an area of economic deprivation with one major industry still providing work. The college had three sites and around 4,600 FTE students. Basic skills support was again a recent development having grown out of ABE services. In 1994-95 more than 295 full-time students received basic skills support which was provided by two full-time and three part-time dedicated basic skills support tutors on two of the sites. Sessional, hourly paid tutors were used on the third site.

The fourth college was a small, single-site rural town college with under 2,000 FTE students. Basic skills support was a very new development and was provided through a Central Resource Unit completely separate from the college's ABE provision. One full-time dedicated basic skills support tutor provided the service to 50 full-time students.

The fifth college was also single-sited and in a small town in a rural county with under 2,000 FTE students. Basic skills support had been established recently and had grown out of the ABE service. One full-time and nine part-time dedicated basic skills support staff provided basic skills support to 120 full-time and 230 part-time students in 1993-94.

The sixth college was a large multi-site (4 main sites and several smaller ones) college in an area of high unemployment which had seen the main industry collapse in recent years. The college had over 8,500 FTE students. Basic skills support had grown out of the ABE service and was a recent development. Five full-time dedicated basic skills support staff, working with 19 staff who taught basic skills support as part of their job responsibilities, provided support to 200 full-time and 300 part-time students in 1993-94.

The seventh college was also in an area of economic deprivation with over 2,500 FTE students. The basic skills support service had been established in the mid-eighties with Basic Skills Agency support and was provided through a Central Resource Unit. Basic skills support was provided by six dedicated staff to 100-250 students.

The last college was on city outskirts serving a wide community with a significantly higher proportion of ethnic minority students than in the general population. The college had over 4,300 FTE students. Basic skills support was established with Basic Skills Agency support in 1991 and was provided through a Central Resource Unit. Three full-time and two part-time dedicated basic skills support tutors worked with six staff providing basic skills support as part of their duties to provide a service to c.200 students.

Student survey

Three sets of interviews with students were held over the academic year 1994-1995 in November, February/March and late May. The research team's intention was to interview 30 students per college; 15 receiving basic skills support and 15 identified as needing basic skills support but not receiving it. In practice this proved impossible at most colleges as basic skills support staff were unable in some cases to identify students who had not yet taken up basic skills support. This was because screening tests had not been analysed by November or because students had only just been referred to basic skills support and had not yet had a session scheduled. In other cases students could be identified but locating those willing to be interviewed was not possible. Students' progression and achievements were collected from tutors at the end of the academic year, along with attendance frequency.

The student interviews focused on socio-economic and educational backgrounds, experiences of college, perceptions of skills, perceptions and satisfaction with basic skills support and aspirations. Interview results were analysed using SPSS-PC software.

Management survey

Managers at two levels were interviewed in each of the eight colleges using semi-structured interview schedules which allowed the interviewees scope for discussion of the topics raised.

These interviews were conducted in November and December 1994 and focused on:

- staffing of basic skills support

- monitoring and evaluation

- cost of basic skills support

- delivery methods

- external networks

- the place of basic skills support in the curriculum

- the place of basic skills support in college structures and planning mechanisms.

None of the managers interviewed could provide the costs of basic skills support at the interview. This was followed up with a written request for information on costs, which yielded very little information. Interviews were mostly tape-recorded and all were written up for analysis by hand.

Teaching staff survey

In each of the case-study colleges approximately five basic skills support staff and five subject teaching staff without basic skills support responsibility were given two survey instruments. The first of these instruments was a questionnaire focusing on:

- nature and availability of basic skills support service offered

- identification of basic skills support need

- subjects studied by basic skills support students on their main programme

- promotion of basic skills support provision

- monitoring of attendance and performance

- teaching strategies used in basic skills support

- perceptions of basic skills support provision.

The second instrument was an exercise aiming to investigate methods used to identify basic skills need, examining consistency between subject and support staff and across colleges (see Appendix II). The exercise contained five extracts of student work with details of grading or performance criteria from the programme for which each student's work was written. Staff were asked to consider three of these pieces of work, decide whether each piece met the criteria given and respond to a series of questions and statements about basic skills in relation to mainstream FE programmes.

Both the questionnaire and exercise results were analysed using SPSS-PC software.

Audit

The audit (see Appendix III) was conducted in March 1995. Its purpose was to gain objective measures of the basic skills support service provided in each of the colleges. The audit examined basic skills support services against criteria derived from the literature and approved by the Project Steering Group. The criteria were in the form of performance characteristics and evidence was collected against these characteristics on a systematic basis.

Evidence collected was coded against characteristics and analysed using SPSS-PC. Each characteristic was examined across sites, by location, through the curriculum process, by type of student and by type of staff. The characteristics focused on:

- promotion/publicity for basic skills support
- identification of need
- availability and accessibility of basic skills support service
- basic skills support provision and level of need
- basic skills support materials
- student progress and achievement
- staffing
- strategies for improving basic skills support.

The documentary evidence collected during the audit was later analysed to provide support or otherwise to statements made by management, staff and students during their surveys.

Presentation of results in this report

This report contains findings from all of the surveys and presents them as one body of research. The report indicates whence results have been drawn in each example, table or figure.

CHAPTER 3

National developments affecting basic skills support

Introduction

During the early 1990s FE has seen large increases in the numbers of students and this has brought more diversity to FE colleges. With this diversity has come an increase in the number of students requiring help with their basic skills to enable them to complete academic or vocational courses. Increased recruitment targets have been met by colleges recruiting 'from sections of the community who have not traditionally participated in education' (Silk, 1994, p8).

Such sections of the community will include:

- adults, to update existing skills or learn new ones in order to work in industries and services requiring new skills, such as IT
- ethnic minority students
- women
- long-term unemployed.

Students from these backgrounds are likely to have low levels of confidence or of basic skills and they may need support to meet their full potential. Students from the traditional FE age group of 16-19 year olds are also more likely to enter college needing basic skills support, since the proportion of this age-group going to college has grown with the decrease in work or training opportunities. For example, the proportion of 16 year olds in full-time education rose from just under 50% in 1983 to over 65% in 1991 (Audit Commission, 1993).

In parallel with this, two other developments have led to an increased focus on basic skills in FE.

1. The introduction of new qualifications – GNVQ and NVQ – in which core skills are an essential part of the GNVQ syllabi and are optional for NVQ. Traditional FE courses, such as A levels and BTECs did not and do not contain such components. FEFC inspectors reported retention rates as low as 30% on a few GNVQ courses and expressed concern about high non-completion rates (FEFC, 1995).

2. National Targets for Education and Training (NTET) have included core skills as an explicit Foundation Learning Target since 1994. (National Advisory Council for Education and Training Targets, 1995).

Since FE colleges were incorporated in 1993, funding has been provided by the Further Education Funding Council (FEFC) on a formula basis which not only considers the number of students recruited but also looks at the number retained through their course of study and the number achieving success in their courses (FEFC, 1994). This has led to colleges having to develop and improve their management information systems to demonstrate numbers of students recruited, retained and achieving each year. Since incorporation, the numbers of students have increased and the sector as a whole has had to make 5% efficiency gains. For some colleges this has meant a decrease in their income per student.

The FEFC funding formula also allocates money for additional support per student, which might be for the needs arising out of physical disability, specific learning difficulties or basic skills. This allocation is not available to colleges in Wales which are funded by the Welsh Further Education Funding Council (WFEFC). Colleges are thus encouraged to provide basic skills support by being able to secure funding to pay for staffing, accommodation and resources.

The development of basic skills support has also been informed by national concern over reports on the high rates of non-completion and non-achievement by FE students. This and other research projects have been commissioned in response to such reports and the concern of FE about recruitment, retention and achievement. The Further Education Development Agency (FEDA, formerly FEU) reported that, 'Colleges are adopting a range of strategies, with most attaching great importance to the need to make early and informed judgements about learners in order to guide them towards, and support them through, the most appropriate learning programme' (FEU, 1994). FEDA itself is supporting work on diagnostic assessment in relation to learner support. Diagnostic assessment and initial screening are being used by more and more colleges to identify students in need of basic skills support and to define the nature of individual student basic skills support need.

In summary, six key national developments have affected the introduction and development of basic skills support services in FE across England and Wales.

1. Increase in student numbers and the need to recruit from nontraditional groups.

2. Introduction of GNVQ/NVQs with mandatory core skills components.

3. Introduction of NTET (1994 onwards).

4. FEFC funding formula (1993 onwards).

5. Concern over high rates of non-completion in FE.

6. Concern over low achievement rates of FE students.

Case-study colleges and national developments

Evidence from interviews with managers and analysis of documents collected during the audit suggested that case-study colleges were developing their basic skills support services in response to these national changes.

Senior managers mentioned all of the six key national developments, except NTET, as key influencing factors on their colleges' basic skills support provision. As NTET are the most recent of the national developments, their influence had perhaps not been appraised and assimilated by the time of the interviews in November/December 1994.

Managers also discussed the place of basic skills support in working towards meeting their colleges' mission statements or equal opportunities policies. Support for students to achieve their primary learning goal was seen as a key part of ensuring equality of opportunity for all. All eight case-study colleges had such equal opportunities policies with some specifically mentioning additional support as part of every students entitlement at college. Clients' or Students' Charters also included equality of opportunity statements and the entitlement to additional support, including basic skills.

The research team also found evidence that colleges were looking at increased recruitment targets in some depth and relating this to basic skills support provision. The national increase in student numbers meant that colleges were recruiting from a more diverse community than previously and it was clear that colleges had considered the basic skills support implications of this. As examples, two case-study colleges' Strategic Plans mentioned as planning assumptions, the increase in 'non-traditional client learner groups' and in ethnic minority and unemployed adults entering college. Both then detailed the need to meet these potential students' needs with expansion of basic skills support provision. One detailed amongst its priorities, 'further expansion of provision of flexible "Learner Centres" and the provision/re-allocation of space for Learning Resource Centres'. The second stated that 'there will be a significant increase in supported student learning' and that they should, therefore plan an 'extension of the Open Study Centre to meet increased requirement by students'.

Six of the seven English colleges were claiming 'additional support units' from the FEFC to fund basic skills support. Some managers, however, mentioned difficulties with funding as a factor in developing basic skills support. Difficulties related to the FEFC formula or to allocations of funding for basic skills support within college.

The case-study colleges appeared to be aware of the demands which national developments were making in FE and were developing basic skills support provision to help meet those demands.

The role of the Basic Skills Agency in case-study colleges' basic skills support development

Evidence collected during the audit and managers' responses to questions on external support for the development of basic skills support demonstrated that the Basic Skills Agency had a national role in informing the establishment and development of basic skills support services.

The Basic Skills Agency was the only external contact mentioned by all managers, who commented that its publications, newsletters, Development Officer contacts and consultancies provided a vital or useful network. They reported that the Basic Skills Agency had been instrumental in developing the basic skills support provision in their colleges. Two colleges had established their basic skills support services through Basic Skills Agency projects. Others had used its consultancy services or visits to the Agency sponsored National Support Project (NSP) at Wakefield College to inform their own colleges' basic skills support provision.

Documents collected during the audit supported the view of managers that the Agency had a national role to play in developing FE basic skills support services. These documents included project and consultancy reports and outcomes of visits to the NSP at Wakefield.

CHAPTER 4

The wider picture of basic skills support in FE

Introduction

This chapter details the main findings on basic skills support provision from the 1994 and 1995 statistical surveys. Data collected from these surveys on completion and achievement are presented and discussed in Chapter 6. Both surveys were of 206 colleges across England and Wales, with a response rate of 137 colleges to the 1994 survey and 80 colleges to the 1995 survey.

Identification of need

Both statistical surveys asked whether screening was used to identify students in need of basic skills support. In the 1995 survey 61% of respondents said their colleges screened for basic skills support need, a slight increase on the 1994 survey. Of those respondents who used screening, most (98% in 1995 and 76% in 1994) screened all full-time students, but very few screened all part-time students (6% in 1995 and 10% in 1994).

This suggests a national picture of nearly all full-time students and very few part-time students being screened at over half the FE colleges in 1994-1995. This picture was reflected in the case studies where management expressed long-term plans to screen all students but in reality full-time students were usually the only ones subject to screening. It is also reflected in the FEFC's GNVQ Inspectorate Report (FEFC, 1995) which found screening of full-time students for basic skills support in about 70% of the colleges inspected.

The two statistical surveys showed a decrease in the reliance colleges placed on external tools for identifying basic skills support need. Tools such as exam results, school reports and Records of Achievement were used by fewer than half the 80 respondents in 1995. A corresponding increase in the use of internal tools (screening and initial interviews) was seen with over 85% of the 80 respondents using them in 1995.

Take-up of basic skills support in the FE community

Sixty-four respondents to the 1995 completion and achievement survey gave the number of students screened/assessed for basic skills support, and the number of those students who were identified as needing basic skills support. A total of 54,124 students in the 64 colleges were screened/assessed of which 16,684 were identified as in need of basic skills support, with a mean of 261 and median of 134 students per college. The proportion of students screened/assessed found to be in need of support was around 30% using either the mean (30.8%) or median (29.3%).

The range varied with six respondents identifying 100% of those screened/assessed as in need. These six colleges all screened a small number of students, from four to 150. It may be that these colleges only screened/assessed those already known or suspected to be in need of basic skills support. The numbers are so small as to suggest that no blanket screening was carried out. The lowest proportion of screened/assessed students being identified as in need of basic skills support was 4.6%.

Sixty respondents gave the numbers of students receiving support and only 54 gave the numbers not receiving it. It is interesting to note that in only 79.6% of the 54 cases where numbers receiving and not receiving support were both provided did the numbers tally to the total number of students identified as in need of support.

Results for the 54 colleges from which responses to both questions were received showed 8,333 students receiving support and 4,918 not receiving support out of 13,796 students identified as in need of basic skills support. The mean proportion of students identified as in need of support and receiving it was 60.4%. Eleven respondents reported 100% of students identified as in need, receiving support and the median proportion was considerably higher than the mean at 73.3%. The reverse pattern held for students identified as in need of support but not receiving it where the mean was 35.6% and median 20.7%. *Table 1* shows the numbers of respondents reporting proportions of students receiving and not receiving basic skills support.

Table 1: **Proportions of students receiving and not receiving basic skills support**

	Proportion of students			
	≤ 25%	25.1-50%	50.1-75%	75.1% ≤
Receiving bss (no. respondents)	3	12	16	23
Not receiving bss (no. respondents)	29	12	10	3

There may have been a number of reasons for students not receiving basic skills support, such as student refusal, but these figures must in part indicate a lack of availability of basic skills support to those requiring it, in a substantial number of colleges.

Staffing of basic skills support

The 1995 statistical survey showed:

- 55% of respondents had staff solely providing basic skills support and 69% of respondents had staff providing basic skills support as part of their duties. The colleges had:

  - a mean average of 3.9 part-time (median of 5) and 2.4 (median of 2) full-time staff working solely in basic skills support

  - a mean average of 4.8 part-time (median of 4) and 4.3 (median of 4) full-time staff for whom basic skills was part of their duties.

Only 31% of colleges in the 1994 survey reported having administrative support for basic skills support.

Models of provision

Both statistical surveys of 206 colleges asked respondents to indicate the structural model which their colleges used in the delivery of basic skills support. Results showed a move towards clearer centralisation of resources with cross-college responsibility apparent. Very few colleges had support structures designed on a departmental basis, with around one-fifth of colleges having a mixture of a departmental system and a Central Resource Unit (CRU).

Figure 1 details the proportion of respondents using each of four structural models of delivery in the 1994 and 1995 statistical surveys.

The change from 1994 to 1995 should be noted here with a move away from basic skills support as an extension of primary basic skills to basic skills support from a Central Resource Unit. This suggests that basic skills support was becoming more established in its own right; having evolved from primary basic skills it was now a distinct part of FE colleges' services.

Figure 1: **Structural models of basic skills support delivery**

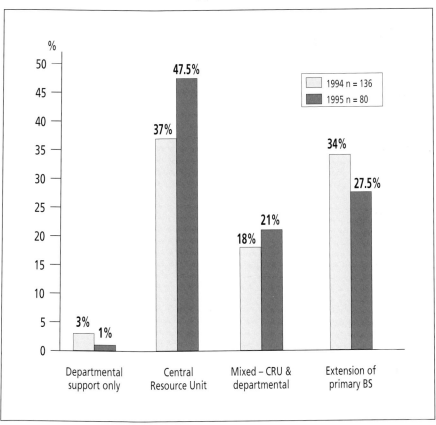

The statistical survey in 1994 based its questions on the venue for basic skills support provision on the assumption that the majority of support would be provided via some kind of central resource unit. The study found that a significant proportion listed 'other' centres for provision. Results from the case studies suggested that much of this 'other' provision was in-class support.

The wider picture was one of most students being referred to a centralised basic skills support unit, either a dedicated unit or one providing basic skills support alongside primary programmes. Roughly one in five students identified as needing basic skills support could expect to be referred to a service provided by either a centralised unit or their own subject department, depending upon the department in which the student was based.

CHAPTER 5

Case studies: policy and practice

This chapter looks at basic skills support provision from identification of need through to progress review and evaluation. For each section it examines both policy, where available, and practice as reported in the surveys and as seen in the documents collected through the audit. All data come from the case-study colleges.

Identification of need

Results from the management survey showed that managers in the case-study colleges clearly saw screening of students at the start of students' courses as the method to identify need. Seven of the eight managers reported that they screened all students or specific groups of students; the remaining one planned to do so in 1995/96. They saw it as the most effective way to satisfy policies of meeting individual student need.

Screening

Evidence collected through the other surveys suggested that whilst screening was the most common method of identifying basic skills support need, it was by no means the only one in use and was not as comprehensive as managers reported and policies suggested.

The audit of the case-study colleges found evidence that screening was occurring in the seven colleges where managers reported it occurred. Analysis of the documents collected during the audit did not clarify whether college policy or practice was to screen full-time or part-time students or those from selected courses.

The model process for screening which emerged was:

- vocational, academic or personal tutors administer the screening test during induction

- tests are either marked by tutors and then sent to basic skills support staff or are sent directly to basic skills support staff for marking

- basic skills support staff analyse test results and identify those needing basic skills support to complete their programmes

- basic skills support staff contact vocational, academic or personal tutors, detailing which students need support and asking tutors to refer these students to basic skills support, giving appointments for each student.

The tests used at the seven case-study colleges using screening were either the Basic Skills Agency Screening Test or adaptations of it. Managers commented that a weakness of Assessing Reading and Maths, the Agency's test, was that it does not include a written piece of work. More recent versions of the screening test do include aspects of writing. They reported that they had devised a short written assignment to be included in the test and evidence was found to support this claim. One written test was 'ten minutes to write on a subject from the list given to you by your tutor or on a subject of your own choice' and a second asked students to write no more than a few lines on why they chose their course and what they hoped to get out of college. When interviewed in November almost three quarters (73.9%) of students receiving basic skills support reported that they had taken a 'screening' test.

Other methods of identifying need

Documentary evidence from the audit suggested that two methods other than screening were used to identify need – tutor referral for students once on course and self-referral. Evidence of tutor referrals of students to basic skills support centres was found along with pro-active encouragement from basic skills support services to tutors to refer students, in the form of newsletters and memos to all staff or groups of staff.

Results from the staff questionnaire survey and the audit both suggested that over 30% of students needing basic skills support were only identified once on programme and after they had submitted assignments. Tutor identification and referral were key tools, therefore, in identification of basic skills support need.

They did not appear to be tools recognised by management or supported by policy, however, both of which stressed screening as the tool to identify need.

Students also reported tutor referral as a means by which their basic skills support need was identified, although some of these would have been referrals from screening test results. In some of the case-studies, screening test results were still not available in November. It is reasonable to assume that some tutor-referrals would have been unnecessary had screening results been available earlier.

The staff questionnaire results showed a considerable consensus of opinion between subject and basic skills support staff on the indicators they used to identify students requiring basic skills support.

The most common indicators were:

- not using Standard English in written work (72%)
- lack of basic maths (53%)
- not translating into written work understanding demonstrated verbally (49%)
- not using Standard English in speech (34%)
- not meeting assignment deadlines (32%)
- screening test results (30%)
- not contributing to work of class (26%).

This consensus was largely supported by the staff exercise where subject and basic skills support staff were asked to examine pieces of student work against specified course criteria and decide whether the student needed support. Each tutor had to select three out of five pieces of work to examine and the results are presented in *Table 2*.

This exercise was developed to investigate consistency between subject and support staff and across colleges in identifying basic skills support need. *Table 2* shows a very high level of consistency between the two types of staff for three of the five pieces of work. These three pieces of work were for lower level courses (GNVQ1, GNVQ2 and BTEC) than the remaining two (GCSE and GNVQ3). Subject tutors were more likely than support staff to rate the GCSE student's work as demonstrating basic skills support need and support staff were more likely than subject tutors to rate the GNVQ3 student's work as demonstrating basic skills support need.

Table 2: **Identification of student basic skills support need against performance criteria**

Performance Criteria	Basic Skills Support Tutors						Subject Tutors					
	Yes		No		Unsure		Yes		No		Unsure	
	N	%	N	%	N	%	N	%	N	%	N	%
GNVQ Level 3 Catering and Hospitality	26	90	2	7	1	3	26	70	10	27	1	3
BTEC Nursery Nursing	30	100	0	0			33	94	2	6		
GNVQ Level 2 Health and Social Care	34	100	0	0			35	100	0	0		
GCSE English	4	21	14	74	1	5	4	36	6	54.5	1	9
GNVQ Level 1 Business Studies	16	94	1	6			10	100	0	0		

Self-referral to basic skills support also appeared to be a significant means of identifying need in the case-study colleges. Almost 30% of staff interviewed reported that student self-referral was the means by which their students' basic skills support needs had been identified. The audit supported this, with 22% of evidence collected on the 'people involved in identification of need' relating to self-referral. College documents suggested that some self-referral occurred at the outset of students' courses from those recognising a need to improve basic skills in general and some occurred when students had specific short-term needs to enable them to complete an assignment.

Students receiving basic skills support reported that they knew they needed help with basic skills support. Just over 62% knew they would need help before they started their course and 75.4% knew once they were on course. Those students with higher exposure to basic skills support, as reported by basic skills support staff, were more likely than those with lower exposure to have reported that they knew themselves that they needed help. This is shown in *Table 3* and suggests that students who recognised their own basic skills support need early in their courses were more likely than those who did not recognise it to attend support sessions on a regular or continuing basis.

Table 3: **Exposure to basic skills support and student recognition of basic skills support need**

Level of exposure	Knew needed help before starting course %	Knew needed help once on course %
No exposure (n = 15)	60	60
Exposure to several sessions (n = 23)	43.5	65.2
Used support irregularly (n = 16)	68.7	68.7
Exposure faded, need stayed (n = 12)	66.7	75
Exposure faded, need lessened (n = 8)	50	75
Regular user of basic skills support (n = 28)	71.4	89.3
Intense exposure (n = 19)	68.4	89.5
Total population (n = 121)	**62**	**76**

The analysis of documents collected during the audit found a report from one college that 60% of the users of learning support in 1993-94 were self-referrals. A number of self-assessment and 'request for basic skills support' forms were also found. In addition to these pieces of evidence, all eight colleges publicised and promoted their basic skills support services in a variety of documents for students. Student handbooks, diaries, prospecti and induction booklets contained references to basic skills support, explaining what was offered and how to get help. Specific leaflets about basic skills support and college posters and notice-boards also served to promote the service to students. This multiple publicity can only have served the purpose of encouraging students to access basic skills support themselves.

Identification of the nature of individual student need

Managers reported that basic skills support was provided to meet the identified individual needs of each student. Screening does not identify the nature of individual needs, except broadly whether the need lies in numeracy, literacy or both areas. Tutor and self-referrals may identify specific areas of need but this cannot be assumed to be reliable, nor can it be consistent or exhaustive, particularly for student self-referrals.

The process for identifying the nature of individual need came after initial identification by screening, tutor or self-referral in the case-study colleges. Results from the Basic Skills Agency Screening test can be related to the programme in which the student is enrolled. A discrepancy between the level of skills students possess and the level required for successful completion of their courses can be demonstrated, but no specific areas of basic skills support need will be identified. Evidence from the documents collected in the audit showed that six colleges were using this method to identify need with a seventh identifying all students who failed to reach Level One in the test as in need.

Managers reported that Individual Learning Plans or negotiated learning plans for basic skills support were drawn up by each student with a basic skills support tutor on the student's first visit to basic skills support. Evidence collected during the audit supported these claims. Students negotiated an Individual Learning Plan with basic skills support tutors either directly after referral or after an initial interview and further assessment carried out by basic skills support staff. Individual Learning Plans detailed learning outcomes and the means by which students aimed to achieve such outcomes.

Availability and accessibility of basic skills support

Policies on availability

Managers all reported that basic skills support was the entitlement or right of every student enrolled in college. Documents collected during the audit largely supported this claim. Student Handbooks, Induction Packs and Charters, amongst other documents, not only mentioned basic skills support but claimed that basic skills support was available to, or a right of, all students. One college's Charter had two separate statements putting this very clearly:

> 'You can also expect: . . . additional support to assess your
> needs and what we can offer, including extra staff . . .'

> 'You can also expect that your Learning Programme will . . .
> offer additional support in literacy, numeracy . . .'

College documents such as Strategic Plans and Equal Opportunities Policies also referred to entitlement to basic skills support.

Availability of basic skills support

Of the items of evidence collected on the availability of basic skills support in the audit, 59% showed college-wide availability and 41% departmental availability. The audit also looked at how accessible services were in different parts of colleges. Accessibility on all sites scored 67%, closely matching the 72% of staff who stated that basic skills support services were available cross-college. It also showed clearly that the service was more readily available to full-time than part-time students.

Analysis of the documents collected during the audit proved inconclusive, particularly on whether basic skills support was available on all college sites. Documents from four of the eight colleges stated that basic skills support was available on all college sites but it was clear from these documents that the same kind of basic skills support provision was not always available on all sites. Small community outreach centres, for example, may have only provided a limited service or some sites may not have provided a central drop-in facility.

Who provides basic skills support?

The documents collected during the audit said little about policies on staffing of basic skills support services. Five of the eight case study colleges had documents demonstrating that basic skills support staff were working with vocational and academic staff to provide an appropriate service. All eight colleges had basic skills teaching specialists.

Managers all reported that their colleges had a basic skills teaching team. This team was often providing both primary and support teaching and included staff who taught both basic skills and a vocational or academic subject. Managers also believed that all teaching staff had basic skills support responsibilities, even if simply in the identification of need and referral elsewhere. This pattern was seen through all surveys. Almost three quarters of subject lecturers interviewed in the staff survey said that they provided some of the basic skills support their students received. This was a high proportion, indicating that subject lecturers recognised both basic skills support need and their role in addressing that need.

Audit evidence showed that basic skills support staff were primary providers, the rest being provided by personal tutors, by subject tutors and by counsellors or non-teaching assistants. The audit also examined whether appropriate staff were adequate to meet demand. Appropriate was defined as being qualified and experienced and the numbers of dedicated basic skills support staff were taken into account. In just over 65% of cases, evidence showed that appropriate staff were adequate to demand on all college sites.

Documents collected in the audit pointed towards increased collaboration between basic skills support and subject tutors, both in developing basic skills support activities and materials and in delivery of basic skills support. Two colleges provided documents with evidence of double staffing of basic skills support sessions, using a basic skills support and a vocational specialist together.

Analysis of these documents, including CVs, also demonstrated that basic skills support staff were experienced teachers with basic skills expertise and that many had the Certificate in Teaching Basic Skills, City and Guilds (C&G) 9285. Vocational and academic staff were being encouraged to take the Initial Certificate in Teaching Basic Skills, C&G 9282/3/4 in three of the eight colleges.

The student survey showed that most of the 104 students receiving support were receiving both on-course support provided by course tutors and off-course support provided by basic skills specialists. On-course support only was being received by 16 students and off-course only by 18 students.

Basic skills support provision

This section looks at the nature of basic skills support provision, examining the kind of support students can expect once they have been referred for basic skills support. It looks at where and how support was delivered and the process of monitoring and feedback to students and to tutors.

Policies on provision

In discussing the delivery of basic skills support in their colleges, managers stressed that delivery was designed to meet the individual needs of each student as identified and negotiated in the student's Individual Learning Plan. Delivery of basic skills support differed from primary basic skills teaching for five of the eight interviewees in this way: primary basic skills programmes were 'class situations' with all students following the same syllabus whereas basic skills support involved working to meet individual goals associated with a primary learning goal outside basic skills. Management perceived basic skills support as inextricably linked to students' academic or vocational programme material and goals.

Managers expressed opinions about this link being easier to achieve with students on GNVQ/NVQ programmes, as the support could be linked to the core skills element of students' primary learning programmes. Indeed, managers reported that for some GNVQ/NVQ programmes, all or most of the students needed basic skills support to achieve core skills requirements and thus gain a qualification. In such cases, basic skills support was taught to groups of students from one programme, as part of the core skills sessions.

Managers reported that basic skills support staff worked closely with vocational tutors to ensure that teaching methods and materials were appropriate to the main programme. They stressed the need for materials and resources used in the delivery of basic skills support to be relevant to students, or vocationally based.

Interviewees expressed concern at the dearth of vocationally relevant basic skills materials, with most reporting that they had developed their own teaching packs. Interviewees were aware that there must be much duplication of effort in developing support materials and expressed a desire for published, high quality, relevant materials. Three interviewees said that they had been able to purchase some materials, examples being in 'Caring Studies' and those produced by the Construction Industry Training Board.

Those colleges devising their own support materials were often doing this in partnerships; some between basic skills and vocational or academic staff within college and some between staff in two or three local colleges.

Managers at all eight colleges reported that they collected attendance monitoring data on basic skills support students. They also reported monitoring student progress in basic skills support.

Managers reported that progress was monitored at six of the colleges by completion of a diary, record book or log of work and outcomes of each basic skills support session. This was completed with a basic skills support tutor and kept with the student's Individual Learning Plan in the basic skills support workshop.

The other two colleges monitored progress through:

- six-weekly reviews by students and basic skills support staff
- basic skills support team leaders assessing student progress.

Managers did not use attendance and progress monitoring data to evaluate effectiveness of basic skills support nor to feed back to their colleges' Senior Management Teams (SMTs). They all agreed, however, on the usefulness of the Individual Learning Plan as a means of reviewing a student's basic skills support progress and as a recording system to demonstrate the work and achievements of each student.

To sum up the managers' perceptions of college policy, they believed that:

- basic skills support delivery was designed to meet individual needs
- basic skills support was sometimes taught to groups of students in a programme area, particularly in GNVQ/NVQ courses where it was incorporated into core skills delivery
- basic skills support was being developed by basic skills support specialists working with vocational and academic staff to develop appropriate methods and materials
- basic skills support attendance was monitored through centrally-processed registers
- basic skills support progress was monitored through the use of Individual Learning Plans.

Analysis of the documents collected during the audit showed very little written policy to support these management beliefs. Student entitlement to basic skills support to meet need, as already discussed, was a key written policy of the colleges but no specific college policies on delivery and review were found. This might be expected in Further Education where specific delivery methods are traditionally the province of individual tutors or teams of tutors. Documents written by basic skills support team members were found to confirm the picture that managers gave, but these were few and none was a college-wide document.

Models of provision

Location of support

Evidence from the audit and staff questionnaire suggested that basic skills support was provided by central units, usually with a physical base or bases (eg. Learning Centre, Skills Development Centre), offering a variety of 'classes'. This evidence was supported by analysis of documents collected during the audit, such as timetables for staff or for classes within the 'Learner Centres', as well as memos, monitoring data and basic skills support reports.

Staff stated that timetabled classes and drop-in centres were available in over three-quarters of colleges. Timetabled classes did not have a specified location but were separate from in-class assistance, reported to be available in under half of respondents' colleges. The audit did not investigate timetabled classes but found that Learning Centres, Workshops or Drop-in-Centres were widely available compared with in-class assistance.

Analysis of documents showed that a drop-in facility was available in six of the eight colleges. Drop-in facilities were not available on all sites of most of these six colleges, being located in Learner Centres on main sites only. For one college, self-access to materials and resources appeared from these documents to be the only method used to provide basic skills support.

Timetabled sessions were also clearly occurring in seven of the colleges although it was not clear in most cases whether the sessions were for students from a single or from varied programme areas. Again, they were not necessarily available on all college sites, particularly at small outreach centres.

The student survey showed that the majority of the support students received was in maths and English and in working on assignments. More off-course support covered maths and English and more on-course support covered working on assignments.

Students also considered that it was important to have a drop-in capability for off-course support. Students receiving maths support were particularly satisfied with this feature where it occurred. *Tables 4* and *5* report importance and satisfaction scores based on seven point scales, where 1 is low and 7 is high.

Table 4: **Importance and satisfaction ratings for aspects of maths support**

	n	Importance mean	Satisfaction mean
Off-course			
timetabled class	34	5.35	5.15
drop-in	34	5.69	6.12
BS tutor	41	6.27	6.17

Table 5: **Importance and satisfaction ratings for aspects of English support**

	n	*Importance mean*	*Satisfaction mean*
Off-course			
timetabled class	44	5.55	5.36
drop-in	46	6.47	6.00
BS tutor	56	6.20	6.09

Teaching methods and materials

Staff were asked to detail the nature of the support they provided. Results are shown in *Table 6*.

Table 6: **The nature of basic skills support provided by subject lecturers**

	All		*Subject staff*		*Basic skills support staff*	
	No.	*%*	*No.*	*%*	*No.*	*%*
Written English	62	17.6	26	18.7	36	16.8
Spoken English	40	11.3	12	8.6	28	13.1
Reading English	39	11.1	5	3.6	34	15.9
Basic Maths	43	12.2	14	10.1	29	13.5
Group Work Skills	33	9.3	18	12.9	15	7.0
Study Skills	56	15.9	25	18.0	31	14.5
Library Skills	30	8.5	14	10.1	16	7.5
Presentation	50	14.2	25	18.0	25	11.7
Total	**353**	**100.0**	**139**	**100.0**	**214**	**100.0**

The staff survey asked a number of questions on the methods used to teach these subjects. Results showed considerable agreement with the management ideal of individualised teaching and the reality of GNVQ/NVQ core skills incorporating basic skills support for whole groups. Basic skills staff preferred individualised methods whereas subject staff preferred group methods, as shown in *Table 7*.

Table 7: **The method adopted in order to meet basic skills support needs**

Method	All		Subject staff		Basic skills support staff	
	No.	%	No.	%	No.	%
Extensions for assessed work	13	5.8	13	31.0	N/A	–
Spoken English support in class	19	8.4	19	45.2	N/A	–
Individually designed activities	46	20.4	10	23.8	36	19.7
Activities subject based for groups	16	7.1	N/A	–	16	8.7
Skills based activities to res groups	18	8.0	N/A	–	18	9.8
Assist groups with assignments	16	7.1	N/A	–	16	8.7
Assist individuals with assignments	33	14.7	N/A	–	33	18.0
Use basic skills support modules	27	12.0	N/A	–	27	14.7
Negotiate Individual Learning Plan	37	16.4	N/A	–	37	20.2
Total	**225**	**100.0**	**42**	**100.0**	**183**	**100.0**

Staff also detailed the reasons for using their chosen methods. Only two reasons were significant: the method was most appropriate to the student(s); the method was the one which students preferred. The student survey results suggest that tutors' methods were both appropriate and preferred by their students. Students highly valued their tutors' help in basic skills support. They considered both on course and basic skills tutors very important to them and expressed satisfaction with both. This importance and satisfaction with staff held true whether the students were receiving English or maths support or both. Maths supported students were more satisfied with off-course basic skills tutors while English supported students were satisfied with both on and off-course tutors.

The predominant strategies used by staff in basic skills support provision focused on group work, communication skills, skill reinforcement and one-to-one tutorials as shown in *Table 8*.

Again, subject staff were more oriented towards group work and basic skills staff towards one-to-one tutorial work.

Table 8: **Teaching strategies used in the provision of basic skills support**

Strategy	Number	Percentage
Feedback	15	7.6
Miscellaneous	15	7.6
Customised worksheets	17	8.7
Strategies for students to cope	18	9.2
One-to-one tutorials	30	15.3
Communication skills	33	16.9
Skill reinforcement	33	16.9
Group work	34	17.4
Total	**195**	**99.6**

Subject lecturers who reported that they provided basic skills support in their classes were also asked if they provided such support to students who had already been referred to the college service. Forty-six per cent of subject lecturers confirmed that they directly provided some form of basic skills support to students who also used the college provision. In confirming why they did this, 18.6% acknowledged that basic skills support was an integral part of the syllabus, 27% suggested that the students seemed to need it and 9.3% argued that the college service did not seem to meet all needs.

Analysis of documents collected during the audit again showed very little written on the practice of staff in delivery methods for basic skills support. It did support findings on materials used, with a number of basic skills support teaching resources, both specific to basic skills and to vocational areas seen.

The audit found that materials to meet support needs were more likely to be available on some college sites than cross-college. It also found that 62% of materials were subject-based. *Figure 2* shows that the spread across subject areas varied enormously, the lowest in agriculture and the highest in business. The variation related to the balance of the curriculum in the colleges.

The remaining 38% of materials consisted of basic skills materials for writing (39%), arithmetic (31%) and reading (30%). The materials showed a bias to full-time students in provision of support.

Figure 2: **Availability of subject related basic skills support materials as audited**

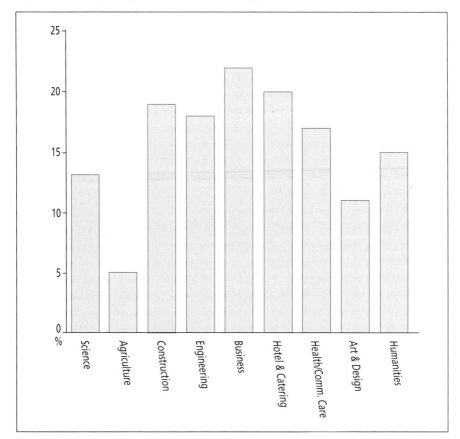

Attendance monitoring

Staff reported the use of five methods for monitoring attendance, with nearly 70% of basic skills staff using registers, concurring with the management view. *Table 9* shows the staff responses, demonstrating that 40% of subject staff relied on student reports.

Table 9: **Means of identifying whether students use the provision**

Monitoring method used	All		Subject staff		Basic skills support staff	
	No	%	No	%	No	%
Progress report from staff providing service	13	13.5	13	24.5	N/A	–
Attendance report from staff providing service	19	19.8	19	35.8	N/A	–
Report from students	21	21.9	21	39.6	N/A	–
Teacher register	30	31.2	N/A	–	30	69.8
Student signing in book	13	13.5	N/A	–	13	30.2
Total	**96**	**100.0**	**53**	**100.0**	**43**	**100.0**

Table 10 below indicates the action staff reported taking with respect to student non-attendance at basic skills support. The majority (57.1%) reported talking to the student. Subject and specialist staff were in communication but, according to subject lecturers in only 18.2% of cases. The views on levels of communication were not shared.

Table 10: **Action taken in the case of non-attendance**

Action taken for non-attendance	All		Subject staff		Basic skills support staff	
	No	%	No	%	No	%
Talked to student	36	57.1	22	66.7	14	46.7
Spoke to staff operating service	6	9.5	6	18.2	N/A	–
Provided support myself	5	7.9	5	15.1	N/A	–
Spoke to personal tutor	16	25.4	N/A	–	16	53.3
Total	**63**	**100.0**	**33**	**100.0**	**30**	**100.0**

Documentary evidence on action to follow up non-attendees was very sparse. Memos from one college showed basic skills support staff contacted students' tutors to inform them of the non-attendees and ask them to refer the students to basic skills support to discuss their needs. Apart from this example, the only other documents suggesting communication between basic skills support and subject staff on non-attendance were progress reports which included the number of sessions students had attended. One college also had an FEFC Inspection Report with comments that it should 'investigate the reasons for poor attendance, especially group support' and that it showed 'patchiness in record-keeping'. The recent FEFC Inspectorate Report on GNVQs in England noted that 'students' attendance at workshops and their progress in basic skills were not adequately monitored or reported to their teachers' (FEFC, 1995). It would appear that the case-studies mirrored the national picture, at least in relation to GNVQs.

Progress monitoring and review

The audit found that progress monitoring was largely available on all sites, predominantly to full-time students and by basic skills support staff. The evidence suggested that in the majority of cases (74%) scheduled reviews did take place, but that 24% of these reviews were conducted by students alone and 60% by staff alone. Reviews covered specific skills (perhaps identified at the diagnostic stage), session aims and programme aims.

Evidence from the college documents collected showed that progress was reviewed through Individual Learning Plans, with a number of examples of completed review sheets and records of work completed, signed by both student and staff member.

The first student interviews asked students to state three things which they hoped to get out of basic skills support. Five clear aims emerged. These were then incorporated into the March interviews when students were asked to rate the extent to which basic skills support had helped to meet those aims. Results are presented in *Table 11* and show that basic skills support was meeting goals to improve work or specific skills but was not seen as leading to longer term aims. Students were asked to rate the extent on a seven-point scale where 1 = 'not at all' and 7 = 'very much so'.

Table 11 also shows that students were reluctant to use the mid-range of the seven-point scale, indicating that they saw basic skills support as either meeting or failing to meet their expectations.

Table 11: **Student aims and extent to which they were met**

	Satisfaction of aim (March)		
Aim (November)	Mean extent to which basic skills support met aims n=112	Proportion rating 1 or 2 (%)	Proportion rating 6 or 7 (%)
Improve assignments	5.5	8.9	76.8
Improve English	5.39	16.1	65.2
Improve Maths	5.29	30.4	64.3
Gain qualifications	4.92	13.4	56.2
Course success	4.49	21.4	34.8

CHAPTER 6

Effectiveness of basic skills support: completion and achievement

Introduction

The research team intended to investigate the effectiveness of basic skills support by collecting and analysing data on completion, withdrawal and achievement from the 206 colleges studied in the 1994 and 1995 statistical surveys, the supplementary statistical survey and the completion and achievement survey of Autumn 1995. Two of these surveys asked respondents to provide the numbers of students requiring and receiving basic skills support, and the numbers who completed and failed to complete their courses. There were a number of problems with the data collected in these surveys so a third one was devised (the completion and achievement survey, Autumn 1995) asking for the same data in more precise terms.

The research team also planned to examine effectiveness of basic skills support in relation to completion and achievement in the eight case-study colleges. The management survey asked respondents about quantitative and qualitative methods used to evaluate the effectiveness of basic skills support in their colleges. The student survey tracked 194 students identified as needing basic skills support through one academic year. At the end of the year the research team collected completion and achievement data along with an indication of each students' level of exposure to basic skills support over the year from the basic skills support co-ordinator in each college.

Responses to statistical surveys

The main finding from all three of these surveys was that FE colleges did not have systems sufficiently sophisticated to track students identified as needing basic skills support through to completion and achievement. Respondents to the 1994 statistical survey indicated that very few colleges had management information systems (MIS) at that time. They also indicated that they planned to collect the data required by the questionnaire in the future, the most commonly cited time was September 1996. The paucity of information in these areas was commented on by the FEFC Inspectorate who stated that 'nationally there is a need for better statistical evidence on retention and completion' (FEFC, 1995).

A number of telephone calls were received from respondents to the completion and achievement survey who were anxious that they could not provide all the data requested. The research team did not log calls but a significant number of callers stated that they were collecting the data requested for the first time in the academic year 1995-96 and would be able to provide it henceforward.

Colleges' lack of available and reliable data for this research can be seen as part of the difficulties FE is having in recording and providing management information. FEFC's external audit of college's funding claims for 1993-94 (the first year after incorporation) showed that more than a third of colleges had failed to keep accurate records on students. Errors included duplicated student enrolments, inaccurate recording of withdrawals and estimated rather than actual numbers of students being used. (Utley, 1995).

The statistical survey data

The May 1995 statistical survey results suggested that two structural models of basic skills support were more effective in identifying non-completion rates. It also suggested that both support as an extension of ABE and support from a Central Resource Unit were at the time more efficient systems for collecting data. *Table 12* shows the proportion of respondents who identified non-completion rates by the structural model of basic skills support in use.

Table 12: **Respondents able to identify non-completion rates by model**

Model	Proportion identifying non-completion % (n = 43)	Proportion in general population % n = 80)
A Departmental support only	2.3	1.3
B Central Resource Unit	51.2	47.5
C Mixture of A and B	14.0	21.3
D Support as extension of ABE	32.6	27.5

The data on both non-completion and achievement provided below comes from the Autumn 1995 completion and achievement survey which concentrated on these two areas and used more precise terminology than the previous surveys. Results show that identified students receiving basic skills support were less likely to leave college and more likely to achieve qualifications than identified students who were not receiving basic skills support.

Caution needs to be taken when generalising from these results to the whole FE sector since the numbers of students came from a small sample of colleges. But the data showed that students identified as in need of and in receipt of basic skills support were less likely to leave college than those identified as in need but not in receipt of basic skills support. The difference between the proportion of supported and unsupported students withdrawing from college was marked, as shown in *Table 13*.

Table 13: **Proportion of students withdrawing from college**

	Number of students withdrawing	Number of students in total	Mean proportion	Median proportion	Number of respondents
Receiving basic skills support	498	4,288	11.6%	8.9%	36
Not receiving basic skills support	599	1,727	34.7%	33%	19

Achievement data showed that supported students were more likely than unsupported students to achieve a qualification or progress to the second year of their courses, as show in *Table 14*.

Table 14: **Proportion of achieving students**

	Number of students achieving	Number of students in total	Mean proportion	Median proportion	Number of respondents
Receiving basic skills support	3,271	4,288	76.3%	86.9%	36
Not receiving basic skills support	755	1,267	59.6%	54%	14

Case-study: completion and achievement

Managers demonstrated a strong belief that basic skills support led to increased success rates, as well as lower non-completion and higher recruitment rates. For most senior managers interviewed, these three factors were crucial in developing, maintaining and supporting the basic skills support service throughout college, as discussed in Chapter 3.

They did not use non-completion nor achievement data to evaluate the effectiveness of basic skills support, although they mentioned that this was becoming of concern to them. Two respondents to this survey had chosen not to evaluate effectiveness of basic skills support in improving retention or achievement rates, seeing the support as an end in itself, not needing any extra justification. Interestingly, these two colleges were the only ones not receiving nor seeking funding for basic skills support; one in Wales where funding is not available and one in England having decided not to seek FEFC funding for basic skills support.

Managers in seven of the eight colleges did report that attendance at, and progress in basic skills support was monitored and the attendance data processed centrally. Analysis of documents collected during the audit largely supported managers' views that whilst retention and achievement of students were primary factors in developing basic skills support provision, data on these factors were not being used to evaluate its effectiveness. The documents also supported managers' reports that attendance and progress were monitored, although it was not clear whether monitoring data were processed centrally or whether they were fed back to students' course tutors.

Findings of the audit itself showed no evidence of National Records of Achievement in use nor of achievement being recorded against GNVQ performance indicators.

Data from the student surveys showed that the higher the level of exposure to basic skills support, the more likely a student was to stay at college and achieve qualifications. This supported management beliefs and reflected the wider picture seen in the completion and achievement survey results.

Students who left reported that whilst they perceived support as helping with their maths, English and assignments, they saw it as less helpful in achieving overall course success and qualifications. However, the most significant findings in the student survey section of the research (*Figure 3*) shows that regular users of support were likely to complete their course (only two with intense exposure left as opposed to 21 with low exposure). The student survey also found that ethnicity, care responsibilities and employment had no significant parts to play in a student leaving course.

Figure 3: **Outcomes and levels of support**

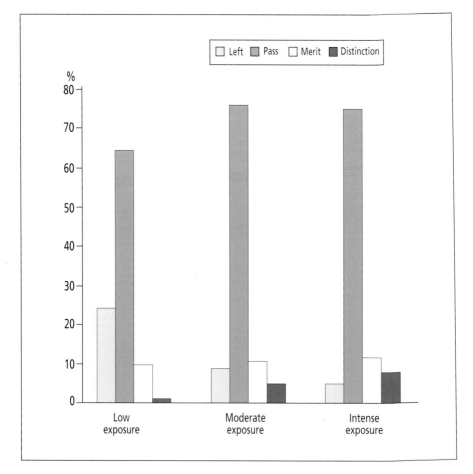

Indications from the student survey also suggested that GNVQ students, especially at Foundation level, were more likely to leave college than students on other courses; 18.96% of GNVQ students left college, compared with 7.86% of students on other courses.

Achievement outcomes, provided by basic skills support coordinators, included actual and projected outcomes. *Table 15* shows the outcome for each student against seven categories of levels of exposure, as reported by basic skills co-ordinators. The Mantel-Haenszel test of linear association found a significant relationship between exposure and final predicted or actual assessments. This demonstrated that the higher the exposure to support, the greater the likelihood of higher assessment.

Table 15: **Exposure to BSS and predicted assessments**

	Left	*Pass*	*Merit*	*Distinction*	*Row Total*
No exposure	16	37	5	1	38.6%
Exposure to several sections	4	15	2		13.7%
Used support irregularly	1	10	1		7.8%
Exposure faded need strayed	2	6	1		5.9%
Exposure faded need less		5	2		4.6%
Regular user of BSS	1	21	2	3	17.6%
Intense exposure		15	2	1	11.8%
Total n	**24**	**109**	**15**	**5**	**N = 153**
%	**15.7%**	**71.2%**	**9.8%**	**3.3%**	**100.0%**

Two other differences between supported and unsupported students emerged from the student surveys; on student self-assessment scores and in self-esteem measures.

All students were asked to rate their skills levels on a five-point scale (1 = poor and 5 = excellent) in reading, writing, maths and spoken English (May only). Analysis showed that non-supported students scored higher in all three areas in November, but by May, supported students were rating their skills higher than nonsupported students. Further analysis found significant improvement in supported students' perceptions of their levels of skill in maths over the academic year. *Table 16* demonstrates the mean rates of supported and unsupported students self-reported skills levels at all three interviews.

Table 16: **Mean ratings of self-reported skills levels**

	November		March		May	
	supported	*non-supported*	*supported*	*non-supported*	*supported*	*non-supported*
Reading	3.15	3.25	3.49	3.65	3.73	3.66
Writing	3.15	3.25	3.38	3.32	3.51	3.45
Maths	2.00	2.60	3.18	2.90	3.34	3.05
Spoken English	–	–	–	–	3.69	3.66

The Rosenthal test of self-esteem showed a significant increase in self-esteem between November and May for students receiving basic skills support.

CHAPTER 7

Conclusions

This chapter draws conclusions from the research, both from the wider surveys and case-study college findings.

The wider picture

The statistical surveys showed that many colleges were not collecting data relating to students needing basic skills support and that management information systems were not widely used.

Particular areas where colleges could not provide data were the numbers of students:

- identified as needing basic skills support
- receiving basic skills support
- identified as needing basic skills support and not receiving it
- who completed their courses and needed basic skills support
- who achieved qualifications and needed basic skills support.

Colleges with a structural model of basic skills support based on a Central Resource Unit or as an extension of primary provision were more likely to provide the data than those with a 'mixed' model of some support provided by a Central Resource Unit and some by individual departments or schools.

A wider picture emerged of most colleges screening all full-time but very few part-time students to identify basic skills support need. Almost a third of students screened were found to need basic skills support and of those identified almost 60% received basic skills support. Students identified as needing basic skills support were more likely to stay at college, complete their courses and achieve qualifications if they received basic skills support than if they did not.

Case-study colleges

The case-study colleges presented consistent pictures in many areas of the research, despite their difference in size, geographical and economic area, numbers of sites and basic skills support history. Basic skills support development was being led by six key national developments:

1. Increase in student numbers and the need to recruit from nontraditional groups

2. Introduction of GNVQ/NVQs with mandatory core skills components.

3. Introduction of NTET (1994 onwards)

4. FEFC funding formulae (1993 onwards)

5. Concern over high rates of non-completion in FE

6. Concern over low achievement rates of FE students

The Basic Skills Agency had a key role to play in informing the nature of the support provided.

Policy and practice in the case-studies

College-wide written policies on basic skills support were largely confined to the areas of identification of need for all students (through screening) and entitlement of all students to basic skills support. In practice, three methods for identifying basic skills support need emerged:

1. initial screening;   2. tutor referral;   3. self-referral.

The nature of students' individual needs was identified through interviews, assessment (other than initial screening) and the negotiation of an Individual Learning Plan.

Other policies and strategies developed by basic skills support managers and supported by the evidence were that:

- basic skills support was linked to students' primary learning goals

- basic skills support was individually negotiated and taught

- Individual Learning Plans were used to negotiate a basic skills support plan linked to primary learning goals

- for courses where a substantial proportion of students required basic skills support, it was provided by course tutors working with basic skills support specialists

- vocational and academic tutors were being encouraged to take the Initial Certificate in Teaching Basic Communications Skills, (C&G 9282/3/4)

- attendance at basic skills support was monitored through registers

- progress in basic skills support was monitored through students' Individual Learning Plans.

Basic skills support was provided through timetabled workshop classes, drop-in facilities and on-course support. Basic skills support was not equally available at all college sites, nor to all groups of students. Full-time students were more likely to have available and accessible basic skils support than part-time students. Most students received support both on-course (usually provided by course tutors) and off-course (usually provided by basic skills support specialists).

Support was delivered by either basic skills support specialists or vocational/academic tutors or by both working together. Basic skills support specialists were not equally available across all college sites. Support specialists were working with vocational/academic tutors to develop subject-specific teaching materials for basic skills support. Such materials were available in almost two-thirds of cases.

Teaching of basic skills support was provided one-to-one (mainly by basic skills specialists) and to small groups (mainly by vocational/academic staff). Staff used the teaching method they believed most appropriate to their students or which their students preferred. Students were largely satisfied with the support they received, both on-course and off-course.

Attendance and progress monitoring appeared to be a weak element of basic skills support services in the case-studies. Attendance registers were kept but little evidence was found on the action taken by staff on non-attendance. Individual Learning Plans were used to monitor progress but scant evidence was found to suggest joint student/tutor completion of progress reports.

The research found that the higher the exposure to basic skills support the more likely students were both to stay at college and to achieve qualifications or progress to the second year of their courses. GNVQ students, especially at Foundation level, were more likely to leave college than students from other courses.

Change and development in basic skills support

Basic skills support was a relatively new service in much of the FE sector when this research project began. In many colleges it was developing rapidly and the research findings demonstrated this development and the associated change and difficulties for FE. College management recognised the need for expanded basic skills support provision, anticipating an increase in the numbers of students requiring support. The research found evidence that expected expansion was being planned for, in the form of extra space and staff.

Managers were also trying to cater for an expanded basic skills support service by securing FEFC funding for supported students. One of the difficulties encountered in funding basic skills support was the lack of data colleges collected on student attendance, progress and achievement. This problem has been documented elsewhere but our research clearly showed that the majority of colleges did not have data on the withdrawal, completion and achievement rates of students identified as needing basic skills support. Many colleges reported that they were developing management information systems. These need to incorporate data on basic skills support need, take-up and progress.

Colleges which had a service providing primary basic skills programmes often used this as the basis of their basic skills support service. The research demonstrated that basic skills support was becoming a discrete service, separate from primary provision. The proportion of colleges using a structural model of basic skills support based on an extension of primary provision fell from 34% in 1994 to 27.5% in 1995. In the case-studies, new posts of basic skills co-ordinator or similar, were often established immediately prior to, or during this research, in the academic year 1993-94.

Colleges were using screening tests increasingly to identify basic skills support need. In the case-studies screening had recently been or was about to be introduced, but was predominantly of full-time students only. The statistical surveys showed that whilst the proportion of colleges using screening tests rose only a little from 1994 to 1995, the proportion of 'screening' colleges who screened all full-time students rose from 76% to 98%. Very few part-time students were being screened for basic skills support need.

The research found that colleges were relying more on internal tools, such as screening tests and interviews, to identify basic skills support need in 1995 and less on **external** tools such as school reports or Records of Achievement. Research findings also suggested that self-referral and tutor-referral were important methods of identifying basic skills support need. Colleges will have to continue to encourage these referrals even as their screening programmes become more comprehensive in order to fully meet need.

Staffing and delivery of basic skills support was also undergoing development. In the case-studies there was evidence that vocational/academic tutors were increasingly being involved in delivery of basic skills support. There was a move towards training vocational/academic tutors in basic skills support tutoring and in some cases they were qualifying in the Initial Certificate in Teaching Basic Skills C&G 9282/3/4. The research found that basic skills support and vocational/academic tutors were increasingly working together to develop appropriate subject-based basic skills support materials and to deliver basic skills support to groups of students from one programme area.

CHAPTER 8

References

ALBSU (1993). *Basic skills support in colleges: Assessing the need.* ALBSU.

ALBSU (1994). *Planning the programmes: basic skills in further education.* London: ALBSU.

Audit Commission (1993). *Unfinished business: Full-time educational courses for young people aged 16-19.* London: HMSO.

Ekinsmyth, C and Bynner, J (1994). *The basic skills of young adults: some findings from the 1970 British cohort study.* ALBSU.

FEFC (1994). *Guidance on the Recurrent Funding Methodology 1994-95.* Coventry: FEFC.

FEFC (1995). *General National Vocational Qualifications in the Further Education Sector in England: National Survey Report.* FEFC.

Further Education Unit (1994). Initial assessment and the diagnosis of learners' support need in *FEU Newsletter* Autumn 1994 pp 13-44.

National Advisory Council for Education and Training Targets (1995) *Review of the national targets for education and training.* NACETT.

Silk, S (1994). *Basic Skills Support.* ALBSU.

TES (1995). Times Education Supplement, 1.12.95

Utley, A (1995). Colleges have to pay back money in *The Times Higher Education Supplement* 20th October 1995. The Times.

Methodology

This section details the methodology used in each of the phases of research for this project.

Phase One: Literature Review

A literature review was conducted at the start of the project.

This involved searching, collecting and analysing research that had been undertaken from 1991 to the start of 1994.

Various approaches to literature searching were used. The three main elements were:

- CD-ROM searches
- paper format abstract and index searches
- visits to special information units.

Phase Two: Statistical Surveys

This Phase consisted of four questionnaire surveys of 206 FE colleges, intended to collect general statistical information on basic skills support.

A consultative approach was one of the key principles upon which the research progressed. Input into the first questionnaire came from the Basic Skills Agency, the Further Education Funding Council (FEFC), Bilston Community College (BCC) and the University of Central England (UCE) through the Centre for Information Research and Training (CIRT). Other individuals were also selected to contribute because of their knowledge of research methodology or because of their specialist knowledge of basic skills within the further education context.

The idea of taking a random sample of general further education and tertiary colleges from the ten FEFC regions, as outlined in the research proposal, evolved into a survey of all general FE and tertiary colleges identified by the Basic Skills Agency as providing basic skills support. Colleges were excluded when provision was limited to only primary basic skills. Selection focused on programmes which had been in place long enough to make a contribution to the study.

The initial design of the questionnaire focused on the different steps a student might face when embarking on a programme of study at a college of further education. Having identified the steps in terms of inputs, process and outcomes the next stage was to design questions that would determine how effective the college systems were at providing basic skills support during each step.

Piloting the questionnaire revealed that a number of questions which identified 'effectiveness' had to be excluded because of the difficulty of obtaining the information. The questionnaire became a tool to identify the systems currently in place and the prevalence of basic skills support in each college. It also assisted the identification of the eight case study colleges.

The first questionnaire asked respondents whether they could identify non-completion rates for students requiring basic skills; 40 colleges reported that they could identify these rates. A follow up survey investigated the numbers of students involved, reasons for non-completion and systems used to identify non-completion rates at these 40 colleges.

A short questionnaire was designed and mailed to the 40 colleges in October 1994. A covering letter asked for responses by 11th November 1994. By the start of December, twelve questionnaires had been returned. A telephone follow-up was conducted with the remaining colleges in an attempt to increase the response rate.

The questionnaire used in the third survey was based on the first and was mailed to the same 206 colleges in May 1995. The questionnaire included the questions asked in the follow-up survey, revised the staffing questions and omitted some questions on resources.

The final questionnaire in this phase focused on withdrawal, completion and achievement rates of students identified through screening or assessment as needing basic skills support. It was devised by the Basic Skills Agency and sent to all 206 colleges in October 1995.

Phase Three: Management Survey

This survey was carried out by interview with two managers having responsibility for basic skills support in each of the eight case-study colleges. One manager was at a senior level, usually a Vice Principal or Director, with strategic responsibility for basic skills support. The second was at middle management level with responsibility for the day-to-day management of basic skills support across the college. Interviews were conducted using schedules, one designed for each level of management. These interviews were recorded for the most part, and transcribed later for analysis.

The interviews lasted approximately forty-five minutes and were conducted in November and December 1994. One section of questions to senior managers asked about the costs of basic skills support. The research team left this section with interviewees, asking them to collect the information and post it to the researchers. A follow-up letter was necessary and six of the eight colleges provided the information required. The results of the survey were analysed, grouping together common themes and drawing out points of agreement and disagreement across the colleges.

There were three main themes:

- policy formation and strategic development
- provision of basic skills support
- evaluation and monitoring.

Phase Four: Student Surveys

The student phase encompassed three structured interviews (November, March, May) with a total of 203 students from the eight case study colleges. All of the students were on full-time courses of study and were perceived by their course tutors or basic skills tutors as needing extra help with basic skills. Support was provided in a variety of forms both on and off the main course of study, which included workshops and drop-in centres, and formal timetabled classes. One quarter of the students reported that extra help was a required, not optional experience. At the end of the academic year basic skills staff were asked to score each student's exposure to all forms of basic skills support. They used a seven point Likert scale with 1 equalling no exposure and 7 intense exposure.

The first interview schedule was piloted at Bilston Community College. Each case-study college was visited by a team of trained interviewers and, where possible, interviews were conducted in private. Some colleges had to be revisited by research teams as insufficient students were interviewed first time.

The November interview required students to identify:

- why they would or would not take up extra help
- what goals they hoped to achieve with help
- the forms of support they were able to access
- personal demographic details.

In the March interview students were asked to rate on a seven point Likert scale the extent to which they felt the basic skills support they were receiving was helping to meet their goals. The May interview looked again at the extent basic skills support was helping achieve goals and looked at satisfaction with support. At each interview, all students were asked to rate their reading, writing and maths skills, to report changes in demographic details, to answer questions for assessing their self esteem and feelings of attribution for success and failure. Students in the sample who left college during the research were interviewed and asked about their reasons for leaving.

Data were analysed using SPSS Windows crosstabs, ANOVAs and repeated measures t-tests where appropriate.

Phase Five: Audit

This Phase involved collection and analysis of data against performance characteristics (see Appendix III).

The college audit form was used by the researchers to collect observed practices. The form was also used to track three students from each college, one from each of three categories, namely:

- students in receipt of basic skills support
- students offered basic skills support but who had not taken up this service and
- students not receiving basic skills support.

A timetable of visits to collect data for the audit was prepared. Colleges were contacted and confirmation provided of the support which they would need to provide to the research teams. The finalised visit period ran from 20th February to 31st March 1995. Each college was asked to provide access to a variety of information relating to the delivery of the basic skills support service. In the event, seven of the eight colleges were able to provide full access to documents, staff, students and the working environment. One college was unable to provide full access to documentary evidence.

Each team of two researchers spent one week at each of the colleges. During that period, four sets of audit reports forms were completed, each set comprising fourteen sheets, one for each characteristic. Approximately three days were spent in gaining a description of the service by completing one set of these forms and collecting the associated documentary and observed evidence. The documentary evidence was logged onto a pre-coded sheet whilst the observed evidence was recorded on a standard form. The last two days were taken up with tracking the three students. The evidence from each student was recorded onto a set of audit report forms.

The first stage in the collation of the Audit was to code and transcribe the results from each of the eight colleges onto a table in order to identify common clusters. The information from the student audit was similarly coded and transcribed. The researchers standardised the way they identified the three students 01, 02 and 03. Comparison between type of students as well as students and staff was possible. The final stage of the audit involved content analysis of the documents collected during the 'audit week' from each college. A list of questions was drawn up, to match areas covered in the other surveys, and documents were examined for evidence on each question listed.

Phase Six: Staff

For this Phase three instruments were prepared. The first two instruments were interview schedules.

One questionnaire was produced for basic skills support lecturers and one for subject lecturers. The first section focused on obtaining a working definition from respondents of basic skills support by establishing a link between The Basic Skills Agency definition and the services provided in the individual colleges. In the second section, factors which might lead lecturers to decide that one of their students needed basic skills support were explored. The level and range of knowledge of the facilities offered by the college was the focus of the third section. In this section, respondents were asked about the interface between course staff and basic skills support staff.

A whole section of the questionnaire was devoted to how both subject and basic skills support lecturers supported basic skills needs of students irrespective of whether they were receiving additional support.

Finally, lecturers were asked to comment on how performance improvement in students was identified and the factors they used to explain this. Respondents were also asked about how they thought the service in their college could be improved.

The fourth draft of the questionnaire was piloted at a college in the West Midlands in January 1995. Ambiguities in a few questions were identified and additional items added to the choice of responses. The final questionnaire was pre-coded.

The third instrument was a basic skills support exercise (Appendix II), produced between June and September 1994. The first draft of the exercise was piloted at a further education college in the West Midlands in January 1995. The pilot indicated that a number of alterations were required, primarily to ensure ease of use. This was achieved through a more structured presentation of the exercise, redrafting of some questions and the addition of 'unsure' response fields to aid the collation of information.

The final version of the exercise was used during the week long audits of basic skills support provision in eight colleges between February and March 1995.

The exercise consisted of two parts. Part A contained five pieces of student work, each accompanied by brief details of the task or assignment which had been given and relevant performance criteria, range statements or grading criteria. Part B contained a series of statements relating to gender, age, ethnicity, previous educational experience and types of support available.

In Part A respondents were asked to select three of the five pieces of student work and indicate whether or not they thought the student had met the performance criteria, range statements or grading criteria stipulated in each case. Finally, they were asked to decide whether each student required basic skills support or not.

In Part B respondents were asked if they agreed, disagreed or were unsure about each of the statements. The pilot version of this part of the survey indicated that some respondents had difficulty replying to the statements because they had not been clustered. To redress this in the final version the statements were categorised into:

- factors relating to students' entry onto programmes
- factors relating to students whilst on programmes
- factors relating to students' exit from programmes.

Selection of Students' Work

The five pieces of students' work in Part A of the survey were chosen to reflect the range of provision commonly found in further education colleges:

- GNVQ Level 3 Advanced Catering and Hospitality
- BTEC National Diploma Nursery Nursing
- GNVQ Level 2 Intermediate Health and Social Care
- GCSE English
- GNVQ level 1 Foundation Business Studies.

Students were asked for their consent before their work was included in the survey. Where possible names were changed to ensure confidentiality.

The five pieces of student work were moderated by an external verifier with substantial experience of assessing BTEC and GNVQ programmes.

In preparation for the data collection, the research team was extensively trained throughout the autumn. Their training covered the following topics: access to the college, negotiation with staff, use of the instruments, recording responses, following up ambiguous or insufficient responses, closing interviews.

Case study colleges were asked to provide names of lecturers who taught in the subject categories identified in the student survey to the research team. One of the colleges was able to comply with this request whilst the remaining seven colleges self-selected the teaching staff to be included in the staff survey. Attempts were made to draw respondents from the same subject areas as for the student survey.

The response rate was high. Researchers were expected to survey ten staff in each college, five who specialised in basic skills support and five basic grade subject lecturers. In total, eighty three questionnaires were returned. However, two colleges returned more than ten whilst one college returned less than ten. The initial analysis of the data showed that the proportions of lecturers from the subject areas were different to the proportion of subjects studied by students. A further sample was drawn of subject lecturers and slightly modified questionnaires and exercises were posted to the colleges. The response rate was excellent.

Seventy-nine responses were received and again two colleges returned more than ten whilst three returned less than ten. In some cases, respondents chose to respond to all five pieces of work and some wrote comments on the exercise, thus providing additional information.

Two programes were written to analyse the data, one for the questionnaire and the other for the exercise. All the data was extracted from the instruments. Most of the questions on the questionnaire were pre-coded and all questions on the exercise were pre-coded.

In view of the role which the case study colleges played in selecting staff for the survey, further information was required to validate the sample. Consequently, two further questionnaires were designed and issued, one to the colleges and the other to the research teams. Questions were asked about who selected the staff to participate in the exercise and the criteria used for their selection. The results demonstrated that the role played by the case study colleges was not significant.

Staff Exercise: Section A

STAFF EXERCISE

Introduction

This exercise has been produced as part of an ALBSU funded research project to assess the effectiveness of basic skills support in further education colleges.

In some colleges, basic skills support may be known as additional support or study support.

This exercise focuses on the core skills of *communication and numeracy* in mainstream programmes which lead to nationally recognised qualifications.

There are five extracts from assignments produced by students in the survey. Each extract is accompanied either by relevant performance criteria and range statements from the GNVQ core skill units or relevant grading criteria in the case of GCSE or BTEC programmes..

You are asked to:

- Consider each piece of work.

- Decide if each piece meets the stated performance criteria and range statements or grading criteria.

- Respond to a series of questions and statements about basic skills in relation to mainstream FE programmes.

The final section of the survey provides you with an opportunity to record any additional thoughts, ideas or comments you may have.

Thanks for your co-operation

GNVQ LEVEL 3 CATERING AND HOSPITALITY

Part 1

Read through the following letter written by a GNVQ level 3 catering and hospitality student. The relevant core skill performance criteria and range statements are detailed below:

Core Skill Performance Criteria

1. The fullness and accuracy of information included is appropriate to the purpose and needs of the audience.

2. The document is legible.

3. Grammar, punctuation and spelling follow standard conventions.

4. The format used is appropriate to the purpose of the material and information is ordered appropriately to maximise audience understanding.

Core Skill Range Statements

Subject matters: Complex and non-routine matters (eg a letter on a sensitive issue).

Format: Outline formats (eg letters, reports, log book entries).

Conventions: Use of full stop, comma, apostrophe, colon, semi-colon, capital letters, sentences, paragraphs, use of highlighting and indentations to enhance meaning.

Audience: People familiar with the subject matter but not in frequent contact with the individuals (eg some customers/clients).

SAMPLE EXERCISE

Director of Personal Training
Europe, Africa, West Asia
Hilton International
PO Box 137
Milbuck House.
Charingdon Road.
Watford, Herts. WD1 1DN

Dear sir or madame,

I am currently studying Catering and Hospitality. I am in my third year at college and second year in GNVQ Level 3 advanced.

Our tutor has recently set us an assignment on International Dimentions. We have to collate information on International Hotel Establishments. I would be very grateful if you could send me some information on:

Careers

Job titles.
Job descriptions of staff.
Job specifications.
Staff responsibilitys.
Rates of pay per hour, salaries, taxation, national insurance, etc.
Promotional Prospects within the company Abroad and England.

Skills needed and gained.

Qualifications needed to work in the establishment.
Qualifications gained.
What is needed to work abroad eg Visas work permits.

Is a language needed to work abroad or does the Hotel provide staff training.

Do the operations differ in Europe to England.

Could you please tell me the career path of the company.

If you have a GNVQ Level 3 Advanced 3 years experience in catering at what position in the staffing structor would be offered.

I have sent some information on the college courses for future reference. I have sent a perpectos and a course leaflet. I hope that you can answer my questions and send me the information to comply with my assignment, please send the information to the above address.

Yours Sincerely,

Marcia Monfies (Miss)

Part 2

Respond to the following:

	Yes	No
1. The student's work is legible.	☐	☐
2. The student follows standard spelling conventions.	☐	☐
3. The student follows standard grammatical conventions.	☐	☐
4. The student's use of punctuation follows standard conventions.	☐	☐
5. The information contained in the letter is appropriate for its purpose.	☐	☐
6. The information contained in the letter is appropriate for its audience.	☐	☐
7. Sufficient information is contained in the letter to accurately convey its meaning.	☐	☐
8. The format of the student's work is appropriate for its purpose.	☐	☐
9. The student has ordered information to maximise audience understanding.	☐	☐

Part 3

Respond to the following:

	Yes	No
The student requires additional support with communication skills.	☐	☐

BTEC NURSERY NURSING

Part 1

The following is an extract from a student's response to an assignment on investigating bullying The task set was to:

'Identify the signs and symptoms of bullying in children'

The assignment is graded at Pass, Merit, Distinction, Refer and Fail levels. The relevant criteria for each level are detailed below:

Pass

Identify the signs of bullying and a basic understanding of children's feelings.

Merit

As above plus show the need for the formation of an action plan, recommendations and a thorough understanding of the subject area.

Distinction

Criteria for merit, plus the ability to combine theoretical issues with practical experience at a level comparable to professionals.

Refer

Little evidence of research.

Fail

Very little individual research and lack of basic understanding of bullying and the issues arising from this.

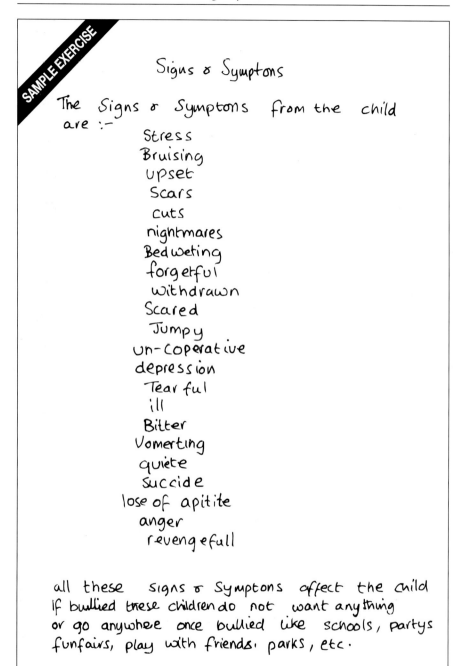

SAMPLE EXERCISE

Signs & Symptons

The Signs & Symptons from the child are :-

Stress
Bruising
Upset
Scars
cuts
nightmares
Bedweting
forgetful
withdrawn
Scared
Jumpy
un-Coperative
depression
Tearful
ill
Bitter
Vomerting
quiete
Succide
lose of apitite
anger
revengefull

all these signs & Symptons affect the child
If bullied these children do not want anything
or go anywhere once bullied like schools, partys
funfairs, play with friends, parks, etc.

Part 2

Respond to the following:

	Yes	No
1. The student's work shows a basic understanding of the feelings of children who experience bullying.	☐	☐
2. The student's work shows evidence of an action plan.	☐	☐
3. The student's work includes recommendations.	☐	☐
4. The student's work combines theoretical knowledge and a practical experience of the issue.	☐	☐
5. There is little evidence of research.	☐	☐
6. The student's work shows little understanding of the issue.	☐	☐
7. The student's presentation demonstrates the need to improve spelling.	☐	☐
8. The student's presentation demonstrates the need to develop assignment writing skills.	☐	☐

Part 3

Respond to the following:

	Yes	No
The student requires additional support with communication skills.	☐	☐

GNVQ LEVEL 2 HEALTH AND SOCIAL CARE

Part 1

Read through the following extract from an assignment on investigating play areas. The relevant core skill performance criteria and range statements are detailed below:

Core Skill Performance Criteria

1. All necessary information is included and information is accurate.

2. Documents are legible.

3. Grammar and punctuation follow standard conventions and words used routinely are spelled correctly.

4. The format used is appropriate to the nature of the material and information is ordered appropriately to maximise audience understanding.

Core Skill Range Statements

Subject matter: Routine matters.

Format: Outline formats (eg reports, log book entries).

Conventions: Use of full stop, comma, apostrophe, capital letters, sentences and pararaphs.

Audience: People familiar with the subject matter and in frequent contact with the individual (eg tutors).

SAMPLE EXERCISE

Investigating Play Areas

After I had visited my chosen play area I found that it
had more bad points than good. The bad points
I have chosen I feel are the worest to make the parte
and the bad langue on the see-saw and all over the
body of the spider, the swings and baby swings were
broken and also the colow is left on a child hand
after holding the side of the swing. The other thing,
are bad are the dogs running loose on there own. I feel
the most bad parte is being by a canal. The park is
full of broken glass and rubbish. all over the frame
of the swing have also got paint chippings
which are very unsafe for small children. The slide
as got very steep step to get up to the top slide.

Part 2

Respond to the following:

                                             Yes   No

1. The student's work is legible. ☐ ☐

2. The student spells routine words correctly. ☐ ☐

3. The student follows standard grammatical conventions. ☐ ☐

4. The student's use of punctuation follows standard conventions. ☐ ☐

5. The information contained in the report is appropriate for its purpose. ☐ ☐

6. The information contained in the report is appropriate for its audience. ☐ ☐

7. The format of the student's work is appropriate for its purpose. ☐ ☐

8. The student has ordered information to maximise audience understanding. ☐ ☐

Part 3

Respond to the following:

                                             Yes   No

The student requires additional support with communication skills. ☐ ☐

GCSE ENGLISH

Part 1

Read through the following extract from a GCSE book review assignment. The students undertaking the assignment were issued with the guidelines on the page after the extract.

Part 2

Respond to the following:

	Yes	No
1. Has the student provided a general introduction?	☐	☐
2. Has the student conveyed the book's theme satisfactorily?	☐	☐
3. Has the student explored the book's characterisation satisfactorily?	☐	☐
4. Has the student made reference to the style of writing used by the book's author?	☐	☐
5. Has the student indicated the audience the book is aimed at?	☐	☐
6. Has the student included their own personal comments?	☐	☐
7. Is there evidence that the student has planned their assignment using the guidelines given?	☐	☐

Book Review

ANNIE

Leonore Fleisher's novel of Annie is a book based on the hit musical of the same title. It as published in 1982 by Columbia Pictures Industries. The book was partly written to make money for the author following the success of the film. It was set in the 1930's in the New York City Municipal Orphanage.

The theme of this novel are like most musicals – hope, love blossoming between unlikely people, revenge, greed and of course everything turns out for the best in the end.

Annie is taken away from the orphanage by Miss Farrell who is Mr Warbucks secretary to spend a week or two with the multi-billionaire as a gesture rather than an indication of his fondness for children. He wants to improve his image. However he eventually becomes fond of Annie and decides he wants to adopt her unaware that she has hopes and dreams of her parents coming to find her. The multi-billionaire offers a substantial reward for Annies parents to come forward.

The climax of the novel comes when Annie's friend from the orphanage prevent Mr Warbucks from being cheated out of his fifty thousand dollar reward.

There are three main characters in the novel: Annie, Mr Warbucks and Miss Hannigan. Athough none of them are realistic, they are entertaining which make the book enjoyable.

Annie's life may have been miserable but she lived in hope. 'The sun will come out tomorrow' because she knew on that outside of the orphanage there was a much better life. Her role is stereotypical she represents all that is good and wholesome, while on the other hand Miss Hannigan is evil and cruel.

Miss Hannigan is one of my favourite characters throughout the book. Although she is portrayed as being the tyrannical, sluttish, alcoholic matron she actually gives flavour to the book. Her role may come across realistically in certain ways but she showed how people can take advantage of their position while caring for other peoples children. However, there is some development in this character, unlike most of the others, because at the end we see that she defends Annie and prevents Rooster from doing his worst with her. The Authur portrays Miss Hannigans character as someone who is lonely and insecure, in the novel she says 'I'd make some lucky man a wonderful wife, but why am I stuck here with sixty miserable, rotten, whiny, nasty, hateful, horrible little girls?'

Mr Warbucks is a man who is arrogant, all-powerful. He has no idea about children, and initially is only interested in making money but in the novel he learns that there is more to life than this. The author shows us in Mr Warbucks character that he was a man that was not conscious of the people around him. In the novel he says to grace his secretary 'I never knew you were so beautiful until now.' We learn more inside into his character as the book progresses that he never knew he had so much love to give to a little girl until now.

The book is written in simple and plain story telling language The writer allows the story to be read by most readers whilst giving them a vivid sense of imagination about the scenes. He has not allowed much action in the book but it is occasionally exiting and mostly cheerful.

The book is aimed at young adults but anyone can enjoy it. It was also written to entertain and to also show how. Annie held on to her dreams to meet with her parents. Unfortunatly her dreams was never fulfill but she found someone to care for her and to show their love for her.

When I was 21 years old I auditioned for a part as one of the servants in the stage play Annie. I enjoyed acting the part, and I went on to watch the film on the television and I found it entertaining. Now I have read the book I find it even better because it it goes into more detail than the film showed. Annie has always been one of my favourite musicals and I certainly would recommend the book to other readers.

Part 3

Respond to the following:

	Yes	No
The student requires additional support with communication skills.	☐	☐

THE ASSESSMENT CRITERIA

Your essay should include the following:

1. An introduction to the work under review

2. An indication of the theme of the work

3. The style of the work

4. The target audience

5. The author's intention

6. The effect the work had on you.

Your essay may include the following:

7. A brief outline of the plot

8. A discussion of the characters.

GNVQ LEVEL 1 BUSINESS STUDIES

Part 1

The following is a student's response to a business studies assignment involving the application of number. Relevant core skill performance and criteria and range statements are detailed below:

Core Skill Performance Criteria

1. Techniques appropriate to the task are selected and used by the individual.

2. Activities required by the techniques are performed to appropriate levels of precision and in the correct sequence.

3. Mathematical terms and mathematical aspects of everyday language are used and interpreted with precision.

4. Use estimation to check calculations.

5. Calculations and results obtained are correct.

6. Aids are used correctly.

7. Conclusions/generalisations/predictions drawn from result are valid.

8. Clear justification is given for the interpretation of results.

Core Skill Range Statements

Techniques:
- Solve whole number problems involving addition and subtraction.
- Solve problems involving multiplication and division.
- Use simple formulae expressed in words.
- Find perimeters, areas and volumes.

Assignment 1

Calculators may be used.

There is to be a refurbishment of some of the offices in a solicitor's practice.

Below is a floor plan of a suite of offices which is part of this centre.

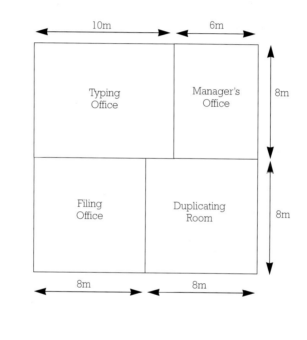

Given that　　**area of room (m²) = length (m) x width (m)**

Task 2a

Calculate the area of carpeting and the length of skirting board required for each of the following:

(a) the Manager's Office, (b) the Filing Office, (c) the Duplicating Room and (d) the Typing Office.

Task 2b

The office suite in question is to be carpeted using three grades of carpet which are:

Imperial	at £18 per square metre
Empire	at £12 per square metre
Tuftex	at £5 per square metre

and Excelsior skirting board is to be used priced at £4.50 per square metre.

Calculate the total cost of carpeting these offices and of fixing skirting board in place using the following grades of carpet:

Manager's Office	– Imperial
Filing Office	– Empire
Duplicating Room	– Tuftex
Typing Office	– Empire

and of course using Excelsior skirting board throughout.

All prices are to have 17.5% VAT added to them to produce a final total cost.

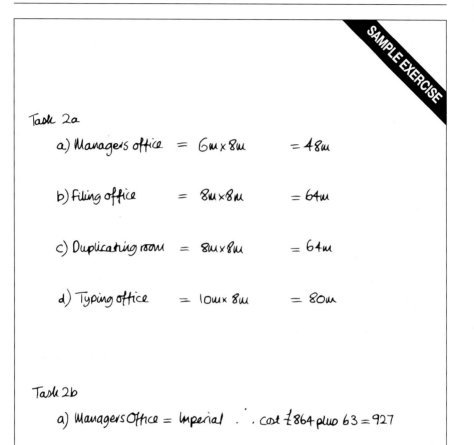

Task 2a

   a) Managers office   = 6m x 8m   = 48m

   b) Filing office   = 8m x 8m   = 64m

   c) Duplicating room = 8m x 8m   = 64m

   d) Typing office   = 10m x 8m   = 80m

Task 2b

   a) Managers Office = Imperial ∴ cost £864 plus 63 = 927

   b) Filing Office   = Empire ∴ cost £768 plus 72 = 840

   c) Duplicating Room = Tuflex ∴ cost £320 plus 72 = 392

   d) Typing Office = Empire ∴ cost £960 plus 81 = 1041

   a) = couldnt do

Part 2

Respond to the following:

	Yes	No
1. The student has selected techniques appropriate to the task.	☐	☐
2. The student has used techniques appropriate to the task.	☐	☐
3. The student has carried out activities required by the techniques to appropriate levels of precision.	☐	☐
4. The student has carried out activities required by the techniques in the correct sequence.	☐	☐
5. The student has interpreted mathematical terms and mathematical aspects of everyday language with precision.	☐	☐
6. The student has used estimation to check calculations.	☐	☐
7. The student has calculated correctly and obtained correct results.	☐	☐
8. The student has used aids correctly.	☐	☐
9. The student has drawn valid conclusions.	☐	☐
10. The student has given clear justification for the interpretation of the results.	☐	☐

Part 3

Respond to the following:

	Yes	No
The student requires additional support with application of numbers	☐	☐

Staff Exercise: Section B

Section B contains a number of statements. Please respond to them by indicating whether you agree or disagree with them. The statements are divided into three categories:

a. factors relating to students' entry onto programmes

b. factors relating to students whilst on programme

c. factors relating to students' exit from programme.

Please respond to the following statements:

Factors relating to students' entry onto programmes

	Agree	Disagree
1. Students who have had positive experiences of education cope well with the basic skills demands of their programmes.	☐	☐
2. The ethnic background of students may have an impact on their level of basic skills.	☐	☐
3. The ethnic background of students has no impact on their proficiency with basic skills.	☐	☐
4. The ethnic background of students has no impact on whether they **seek** extra help with their communication and numeracy skills.	☐	☐
5. Students whose first language is not English may need **extra** help to cope with the communication demands of their programmes.	☐	☐
6. Older students find it easier to seek extra help with the basic skills aspects of their programmes.	☐	☐

Please respond to the following statements:

Factors relating to students' entry onto programme

	Agree	Disagree
7. **Female** students find it easier to ask for extra help with their basic skills.	☐	☐
8. Previous, negative, experiences of education can have a detrimental impact on students' confidence with basic skills.	☐	☐
9. Previous educational experience has little impact on the basic skills performance of students.	☐	☐
10. The gender of students affects whether or not they seek help with the basic skills demands of their programme.	☐	☐
11. Younger students are more aware of the range of extra help with basic skills which is available to them.	☐	☐
12. Younger students need less help with the basic skills demands of their programme.	☐	☐
13. Older students are more embarrassed about experiencing difficulties with the basic skills demands of their programmes.	☐	☐

Factors relating to students whilst on programme

14. Some students lack the basic skills necessary to undertake their programmes successfully.	☐	☐
15. Students need to be taught the communication and numeracy skills appropriate to their programme.	☐	☐
16. Students who need additional help with their communication and numeracy skills should have extra timetabled sessions as part of their mainstream programme.	☐	☐
17. Without some basic skills support some students would not cope with the academic requirements of their programmes.	☐	☐
18. Students find it easier to seek extra help with numeracy than with communication skills.	☐	☐

Please respond to the following statements:

Factors relating to students whilst on programme

	Agree	Disagree
19. Some students are enrolled at an inappropriate level and do not have the opportunity to change programme.	☐	☐
20. Students who find numeracy difficult should be allowed to use calculators.	☐	☐
21. Students find numeracy more difficult than communication skills.	☐	☐
22. Students respond positively to offers of basic skills support.	☐	☐
23. Basic skills support for mainstream programmes is not well regarded by students.	☐	☐
24. Basic skills support is not available on a regular enough basis to be of any significant help to students.	☐	☐

Factors relating to students' exit from programme

	Agree	Disagree
25. Students who do not make use of the basic skills support available to them achieve lower grades than otherwise possible.	☐	☐
26. Students who do not use basic skills support often don't complete their programmes.	☐	☐
27. Students who do not use basic skills support are less able/confident to progress to further study.	☐	☐
28. Making use of basic skills support has no effect on whether a student remains on programme.	☐	☐
29. Making use of basic skills support has no effect on whether a student achieves appropriate grades.	☐	☐
30. Students often comment favourably on the basic skills support they have received.	☐	☐

Audit Instrument

Number 1: **Characteristic: Opportunities for students to find out about the basic skills support service**

	Site								Location						Curriculum Process								Type of Student		Type of Staff				
	Only/ All Sites	Some Sites	Off-site/ Outreach	Recept-ion	Student Services	Skill/ Learning Centres	Work-shop	Drop-in Centre	Student Records	Other	Pre Admission	During Admission	Induction	After Qualifi-cation aim finalised	On Pro-gramme	On-course Assess-ment	Other	Full-time	Part-time	Personal Tutor	Subject Tutor	Basic Skill Staff	Student Counsel-lor	Other
College Prospectus																								
Targeted Information																								
Student Handbook																								
Course Leaflet																								
BSS Leaflets																								
Advice/Guidance																								
Clearly Printed Signs																								
Posters																								
Direct Questions																								
Audio-Tapes																								
Tutorials																								
Other (please specify)																								

Comments:

Number 2: **Characteristic: Opportunities for staff to find out about the basic skills support in the college**

	Site								Location						Curriculum Process							Type of Student		Type of Staff					
	Only/ All Sites	Some Sites	Off-site/ Outreach	Recept-ion	Student Services	Skill/ Learning Centres	Work-shop	Drop-in Centre	Student Records	Other	Pre Admission	During Admission	Induction	After Qualifi-cation aim finalised	On Pro-gramme	On-course Assess-ment	Other	Full-time	Part-time	Personal Tutor	Subject Tutor	Basic Skill Staff	Student Counsel for	Other
College Prospectus																								
Targeted Information																								
Staff Handbook																								
Staff Induction Programme																								
In-service Training within Sections																								
Networking (informal)																								
Newsletter																								
Management Groups																								
Working Parties																								
Team Meetings																								
Central Point of Contact																								
Posters																								
Other (please specify)																								

Comments:

Number 3: Characteristic: Opportunities for the basic skills support needs of applicants to be identified

	Site			Location							Curriculum Process							Type of Student		Type of Staff				
	Only/All Sites	Some Sites	Off-site/Outreach	Recept-ion	Student Services	Skill/Learning Centres	Work-shop	Drop-in Centre	Student Records	Other	Pre Admission	During Admission	Induction	After Qualification finalised	On Pro-gramme	On-course Assess-ment	Other	Full-time	Part-time	Personal Tutor	Subject Tutor	Basic Skill Staff	Student Counsellor	Other
Standard system for college																								
Different systems used by different sections																								
Diagnostic Tests																								
School Reports/File from school																								
Report/File from other Source																								
APL																								
Referral/Identified by:																								
Student (self)																								
Personal Tutor																								
Subject Teacher																								
Specialist Adviser(s)																								
College Counsellor																								
BSS Tutor																								
Advice and Guidance																								
Other (please specify)																								

Comments:

Number 4: **Characteristic: Basic skills support service is available to identified students**

	Site			Location							Curriculum Process							Type of Student		Type of Staff				
	Only/All Sites	Some Sites	Off-site/Outreach	Reception	Student Services	Skill/Learning Centres	Work-shop	Drop-in Centre	Student Records	Other	Pre Admission	During Admission	Induction	After Qualification aim finalised	On Programme	On-course Assessment	Other	Full-time	Part-time	Personal Tutor	Subject Tutor	Basic Skill Staff	Student Counsellor for	Other
Type of BSS service:																								
Central College																								
Departmental																								
Vocational classes																								
Other (please specify)																								
College subject areas:																								
Science																								
Agriculture																								
Engineering																								
Business																								
Hotel and Catering																								
Health Community Care																								
Art and Design																								
Humanities																								
Other (please specify)																								

Comments:

Number 5: Characteristic: Basic skills support service is accessible to those identified

	Site			Location							Curriculum Process							Type of Student		Type of Staff				
	Only/ All Sites	Some Sites	Off-site/ Outreach	Recept-ion	Student Services	Skill/ Learning Centres	Work-shop	Drop-in Centre	Student Records	Other	Pre Admission	During Admission	Induction	After Qualification finalised	On Pro-gramme	On-course Assess-ment	Other	Full-time	Part-time	Personal Tutor	Subject Tutor	Basic Skill Staff	Student Counsellor	Other
Standard college system for informing students																								
Systems vary and only exist for some sections																								
Service available to: 16-19																								
Adult																								
Evening Classes																								
Weekend																								
Employment Released																								
Where is the service provided:																								
Within Vocational/ Academic classes																								
Other (please specify)																								

Comments:

Number 6: **Characteristic:** Basic skills support is provided to the level of need

	Site			Location							Curriculum Process							Type of Student		Type of Staff				
	Only/All Sites	Some Sites	Off-site/Outreach	Recept-ion	Student Services	Skill/Learning Centres	Work-shop	Drop-in Centre	Student Records	Other	Pre Admission	During Admission	Induction	After Quali-fication aim finalised	On Pro-gramme	On-course Assess-ment	Other	Full-time	Part-time	Personal Tutor	Subject Tutor	Basic Skill Staff	Student Counsel-lor	Other
Guidance time identified through:																								
Staff timetable																								
Student records																								
Other (please specify)																								
Records shows:																								
Qualificational held at entry																								
Diagnostic Test used																								
Interview (includes)																								
Nature of support discussed																								
Take up date for support																								
Students perception of need																								
Interviewers perception of need																								
Agreed timed action plan																								
Students signed agreement																								
Other (please specify)																								

Comments:

Number 7: Characteristic: Basic Skills support is delivered in a timely manner

	Site					Location					Curriculum Process							Type of Student		Type of Staff				
	Only/All Sites	Some Sites	Off-site/Outreach	Reception	Student Services	Skill/Learning Centres	Work-shop	Drop-in Centre	Student Records	Other	Pre Admission	During Admission	Induction	After Qualification aim finalised	On Pro-gramme	On-course Assessment	Other	Full-time	Part-time	Personal Tutor	Subject Tutor	Basic Skill Staff	Student Counsel for	Other
Formal system exists for tracking:																								
All students																								
Some students																								
Systems exist for some sections																								
Informal systems exist																								
What triggers the system:																								
Student																								
Personal Tutor																								
Subject Tutor																								
BSS Staff																								
Other (please specify)																								
BSS need is identified																								
BSS begins																								
Records are duplicated and sent to/kept by:																								
BSS staff																								
Personal Tutor																								
Relevant subject tutor																								
Student records																								
Individual students																								
Other (please specify)																								

Comments:

Number 8: **Characteristic: Basic skills support service offers a range of delivery to meet the needs of identified students**

	Site		Location								Curriculum Process							Type of Student		Type of Staff				
	Only/All Sites	Some Sites	Off-site/Outreach	Recept-ion	Student Services	Skill/Learning Centres	Work-shop	Drop-in Centre	Student Records	Other	Pre Admission	During Admission	Induction	After Qualifi-cation aim finalised	On Pro-gramme	On-course Assess-ment	Other	Full-time	Part-time	Personal Tutor	Subject Tutor	Basic Skill Staff	Student Counsel-lor	Other
Individual tutorials																								
Students grouped by:																								
Ability																								
Skill to be studied																								
Qualification aim																								
In-class support																								
Other (please specify)																								

Comments:

Number 9: Characteristic: Appropriate basic skills support materials are provided

	Site			Location							Curriculum Process							Type of Student		Type of Staff				
	Only/All Sites	Some Sites	Off-site/Outreach	Reception	Student Services	Skill/Learning Centres	Work-shop	Drop-in Centre	Student Records	Other	Pre Admission	During Admission	Induction	After Qualification aim finalised	On Programme	On-course Assessment	Other	Full-time	Part-time	Personal Tutor	Subject Tutor	Basic Skill Staff	Student Counsellor	Other
BSS based arithmetic																								
BSS based reading																								
BSS based writing																								
Subject specific support materials in:																								
Science																								
Agriculture																								
Engineering																								
Business																								
Hotel and Catering																								
Health Community Care																								
Art and Design																								
Humanities																								
Materials relate to NVQ level																								
Materials are appropriate to students qualification aim																								
Other (please specify)																								

Comments:

Number 10: **Characteristic: Individual student's progress is reviewed**

	Site			Location							Curriculum Process							Type of Student		Type of Staff				
	Only/ All Sites	Some Sites	Off-site/ Outreach	Recept-ion	Student Services	Skill/ Learning Centres	Work-shop	Drop-in Centre	Student Records	Other	Pre Admission	During Admission	Induction	After Qualifi-cation aim finalised	On Pro-gramme	On-course Assess-ment	Other	Full-time	Part-time	Personal Tutor	Subject Tutor	Basic Skill Staff	Student Counsel-lor	Other
Formal system for regular review																								
Irregular reviews																								
Progress logged by:																								
Student																								
Staff																								
Jointly																								
Progress logged against aims for:																								
Programme																								
Session																								
Specific Skills																								
Action Set																								
Action Taken																								
Other (please specify)																								

Comments:

Number 11: **Characteristic:** Individual student's achievement is acknowledged

	Site										Curriculum Process							Type of Student		Type of Staff				
	Only/All Sites	Some Sites	Off-site/Outreach	Reception	Student Services	Skill/Learning Centres	Work-shop	Drop-in Centre	Student Records	Other	Pre Admission	During Admission	Induction	After Qualification aim finalised	On Programme	On-course Assessment	Other	Full-time	Part-time	Personal Tutor	Subject Tutor	Basic Skill Staff	Student Counsellor or	Other
Qualifications:																								
AEB Basic Skills Tests																								
AEB Achievement Tests																								
C&G Numeracy																								
C&G Wordpower																								
C&G Numberpower																								
Pitman: English for Office Skills																								
RSA English Language																								
RSA CLAH																								
RSA Application Technology																								
Other (please specify)																								
Result conveyed to:																								
Student record																								
Student																								
Personal Tutor																								
Other (please specify)																								

Comments:

Number 12: **Characteristic: Appropriate staff are adequate to demand**

	Site				Location						Curriculum Process							Type of Student		Type of Staff				
	Only/All Sites	Some Sites	Off-site/Outreach	Reception	Student Services	Skill/Learning Centres	Work-shop	Drop-in Centre	Student Records	Other	Pre Admission	During Admission	Induction	After Qualification aim finalised	On Programme	On-course Assessment	Other	Full-time	Part-time	Personal Tutor	Subject Tutor	Basic Skill Staff	Student Counsellor	Other
BSS Service Timetables																								
Monitored Student Attendance																								
Staff providing BSS are:																								
Qualified																								
Experienced (yrs)																								
Other (please specify)																								

Comments:

Number 13: **Characteristic: Unmet demand is quantified and a planned response is available**

	Site									Location							Curriculum Process							Type of Student		Type of Staff				
	Only/All Sites	Some Sites	Off-site/Outreach	Recept-ion	Student Services	Skill Learning Centres	Work-shop	Drop-in Centre	Student Records	Other							Pre Admission	During Admission	Induction	After Qualification aim finalised	On-Programme	On-course Assessment	Other	Full-time	Part-time	Personal Tutor	Subject Tutor	Basic Skill Staff	Student Counsellor	Other
By department																														
By college																														
By type of student																														
By type of course																														
By type of skill																														
By year																														
By person																														
Written plan																														
Verbal report																														
Resource needs specified																														
Staff needs specified																														
Accommodation needs specified																														
Other (please specify)																														

Comments:

Number 14: **Characteristic:** Failure to achieve is quantified and a planned response is available

	Site								Location							Curriculum Process								Type of Student			Type of Staff				
	Only/ All Sites	Some Sites	Off-site/ Outreach	Recept-ion	Student Services	Skill/ Learning Centres	Work-shop	Drop-in Centre	Student Records	Other		Pre Admission	During Admission	Induction	After Qualifi-cation aim finalised	On Pro-gramme	On-course Assess-ment	Other		Full-time	Part-time	Personal Tutor	Subject Tutor	Basic Skill Staff	Student Counsel for	Other
Total number of students identified as:																										
Needing BSS is known																										
Receiving BSS is known																										
Achievement on programme is known within:																										
Courses																										
Department																										
College																										
Course plan																										
Department plan																										
College plan																										
Plans written																										
Other (please specify resources required)																										

Comments: